Breed S
for the R

Colour
Black with clearly defined markings. Colour of markings from rich tan to mahogany and should not exceed 10 per cent of body colour.

General Appearance
Above average size, stalwart dog. Correctly proportioned, compact and powerful form, permitting great strength, manoeuvrability and endurance.

Tail
Customarily docked at first joint, it is strong and not set too low.

Hindquarters
Upper thigh not too short, broad and strongly muscled. Lower thigh well muscled at top, strong and sinewy below. Strength and soundness of hock highly desirable.

Coat
Consists of top coat and undercoat. Long or excessively wavy coat highly undesirable.

Feet
Strong, round and compact with toes well arched...toenails short, dark and strong.

Photo credits:

Norvia Behling
Carolina Biological Supply
Liza Clancy
Isabelle Francais
James Hayden-Yoav
James R. Hayden, RBP
Carol Ann Johnson

Dwight R. Kuhn
Dennis Kunkel
Nancy Liguori
Phototake
Jean Claude Revy
Alice Roche
C. James Webb

Illustrations by Renée Low

INTERPET
PUBLISHING
Vincent Lane, Dorking, Surrey RH4 3YX England

Rottweiler

◇

by Wilhelm Jönas

Table of Contents

ISBN 13: 978 0 966859 22 5
ISBN 10: 0 966859 22 7

The Rott-weiler's unique colouration and high level of trainability have made the breed one of the world's most recog-nisable and popular.

Ancestry of the Rottweiler

No matter how long I am owned by Rottweilers, I will always be fascinated by the unique rust markings over every dog's eyes and on the cheeks. I have been an impassioned student of the breed, its breeding, pedigrees, genetics and history, and still I am fascinated. In Australia, as I learned on a visit there, the eye marks are called 'pips,' a charming and typically Aussie name for these marks! I know that many other breeds have distinctive colour markings, but our Rottweiler stands out amongst the crowd, especially since he stands so tall and proud, as befits his remarkable German heritage.

It is my wish that this introduction to the Rottweiler breed could begin with a definitive statement to show the genesis of the breed. I wish I could pinpoint one breeder (of course in the small town of Rottweil, Germany) who created the breed and show the beginning Rottweiler owner exactly how the great breed began—perhaps even explaining how the pips were born—but it is not possible. As with most other breeds

Rottweilers are great herding dogs and are used extensively by many sheep farmers.

Rottweilers all over the world have the same basic appearance. This is a German-bred dog.

that have been around for more than a century, the exact origins are not known.

THE BREED IN THE FATHERLAND
Most historians trace the Rottweiler back to the invasion of Germany by the Romans who crossed the Alps during the first century A.D. Whether the dogs the Romans used were the ancestors of today's Rottweiler cannot be definitely known, though their chosen canine was said

It was only in the nineteenth century that humans really took notice of the dogs around them, and how they looked, what colour they were and how tall they were. Dogs all along have been helpmates—some dogs hunted, some dogs killed vermin and some dogs protected the property. No one bred the big black dog to the big black bitch because they were both black and big, necessarily. More than likely, humans paired dogs for their abilities. To produce a strong, protective dog, they would mate two dogs with those desirable qualities. Thus were progenerated various dogs with superior abilities.

to be a protective dog that also possessed herding abilities—a description that well suits our Rottweiler. The Romans occupied Germany for no less than two centuries, and their established city there was called *das Rote Wil*, from which the breed's current name derives. Further credit-

ing this theory, early historians cite that direct descendants of the breed lived in areas of Germany that were accessible to the roads built by the Germans in that period.

That said, it is evident that the Romans did not arrive with the handsome black-and-mahogany guard dog we know today, though it is probable the mastiff-type dog they employed, combined with existing dogs in Germany during the first few centuries A.D., formed the basis for today's Rottweiler. That the Romans venerated the mastiff-type dogs, known as

Molossus, is well documented. *Cave canum* (beware of the dog) is an ancient Latin saying that was posted anywhere the Molossus dwelled. Much like today, similar signs are posted. My favourite, which I have seen in England and America, shows the silhouette of a Rottweiler and reads, 'I can make it to the gate in three seconds, can you?' Surely a daunting thought for a would-be intruder! The Romans employed these mastiffs for protection and military work as well as the popular sport of dog fighting. More than one of the Rottweiler's ancestors were lost in the famous Colosseum in Rome;

The Romans brought the Rottweiler to Germany in the first century A.D.

today only the shell of the great arena stands as a reminder of the potential cruelty of humankind to animals and to one another.

The Rottweiler's markings are one of the breed's defining characteristics. Look at the similarity between these three dogs.

This action shot shows some of the problems with which Rottweilers have to deal. Rottweilers, while very strict disciplinarians with their flocks, rarely injure the animals left in their trust.

Also important to ancient Rome were the drover dogs, dogs used to drive cattle over long distances. The Rottweiler's ancestors are believed

Julius Caesar used Rottweilers as guard dogs.

to have been employed by Julius Caesar, one of Rome's great emperors. It was Caesar's notion that his armies should have fresh meat to eat, instead of merely old-fashioned salted portions. The method whereby his

soldiers found their ration of meatballs and bracciole was to have the cattle go to the men on hoof, thus requiring a strong dog to manoeuvre the livestock with skill, grace and speed. The droving abilities of the Rottweiler, even today, speak well of these dogs' innate skill.

During the eighth century A.D., the city of Rottweil, Germany was born. The word *Rote* (as in *das Rote Wil*) referred to the red colouration of the tiles and bricks that were used in the construction of the city. These red tiles were dug up from buildings that collapsed, dating back to the Roman occupation of Germany some 500 years prior. The

Rottweilers enjoy playing with kids...and kids' toys! Be careful though, vinyl toys are dangerous.

The city of Rottweil, Germany is credited as the basis for the name of the Rottweiler. A citizen of Rottweil is also called a Rottweiler in both English and German.

city of Rottweil was exceptional for the high esteem with which it held its dog, in a time when Germans did not consider dogs much more than tools and helpers.

As a helper in Rottweil, the breed became known as a butcher's dog, or, in German, *Metzgerhund*, driving cattle to and from market, the very trait that Caesar employed from the Roman armies. The dogs were tough, fearless and tireless, and rarely backed down from a confrontation with a bull or another dog. Dog fights amongst these butcher's dogs became somewhat common, and any dog with a record of biting had to be muzzled.

The breed's decline was instigated by the government's outlawing of cattle droving, whereby the more industrialised society was finding other methods of moving livestock with wagons and mules.

The Rottweiler likely has close cousins in Switzerland. It is believed that many of the Italian mastiffs, en route to Germany, were left in Switzerland as they crossed the Alps. The Greater Swiss Mountain Dog is a smooth-coated black dog, a bit taller and with different pips. Its three Swiss brethren include the Bernese Mountain Dog, Appenzeller and Entelbucher.

Who could imagine that a breed beginning the twentieth century with such a shoddy representation would finish the century as one of the world's most popular dogs? Never before has such a large and powerful dog become so unbelievably popular around the world. In the U.S., for example, the Rottweiler climbed the ranks to become the number-two dog in the country (in terms of annual registrations as recorded by the American Kennel Club). The breed actually overcame such long-standing popular companion dogs as the Golden Retriever, German Shepherd Dog and Poodle!

Additionally, the threat of wild animals, such as bears and boars, had nearly disappeared. By and large, the Rottweiler was 'downsized' (in modern-day terminology) and the breed nearly fell into extinction. Concerned German dog lovers rescued the breed, which had dwindled down to one dog in Rottweil by the year 1905.

When the Deutscher Rottweiler Klub (DRK) was formed in the year 1907, it was the first breed club for the Rottweiler in Germany. As dog politics are no smoother than government politics, a second club was formed the very same year called the International Rottweiler Klub (IRK). Just 12 years later a third club, the South German Rottweiler

Breed representatives from different countries—here is a German-bred Rottweiler, while the facing page shows an English-bred dog.

A beautifully proportioned and marked English Rottweiler.

Club, was created, and confusion and cantankerous politics reigned. Fortunately, for both German Rottweiler owners and students of the breed, the DRK and IRK did the sensible thing and combined to

Rottweilers can be trained as herders, attack dogs and tracking dogs.

form the Allgemeiner Deutscher Rottweiler Klub (ADRK) in 1921, which absorbed the South German club within three short years.

While it was advantageous to have only one club in Germany, and therefore one stud book to refer to, the Rottweilers already were varying in type, some with weaker heads. Greater uniformity of confor-

The first standard drafted for the Rottweiler occurred in 1901. This description was a joint standard for the Rottweiler and Leonberger. It did not gain wide acceptance in Germany.

mation and sounder construction became the unanimous goal of the new club and the breed was soon appearing more consistent with superior temperaments and work abilities. The club did not sacrifice type, keeping in mind the original droving dogs and their traits. It should be noted that the ADRK

made a conscious decision regarding the colour desirable for the Rottweiler. While the black and rust coloration was predominant, there were other colours as well, including tan and beige, plus some white markings. The selection of the black and rust colouration by the ADRK meant that only dogs of the desirable colouration would be approved for breeding.

Since cattle droving had become nonexistent for the breed, new employment was required. This brought about the beginning of Schutzhund in 1930. This working degree tested the dog's protective abilities, intelligence and training. It became the desired litmus test for breeding stock in Germany and a requirement for Rottweilers to be respected as champions. In addition to attack training, Schutzhund also embraces tracking, basic obedience, the dog's steadiness and willingness to obey commands.

The ADRK standard for the Rottweiler was first adopted in Germany during the early part of the twentieth century; it has remained virtually unaltered over the years, speaking highly of the consistency of the Rottweiler's conformation and temperament.

THE ROTTWEILER IN THE U.K.
The first Rottweiler to enter Great Britain did so in 1936, imported by fancier Thelma Gray. The first bitch was named Diana v.d. Amalienburg, SchH I, whom she sold to Mrs. Sim-

mons of the Crowsteps prefix. The second Rottweiler, also a bitch, was Enne v. Pfalzgau, bred by Herr Weinmann, a good winning three-year-old German dog. She was said to have a weak head that she passed to her progeny. She was sold to

von Kohlerwald—some of which did well at the shows but were sent to Ireland during the war and were never seen again. Miss Homan imported Benno von Kohlerwald, who did not do well in quarantine and had a shaky temperament once

The Rottweiler has gained a devoted following in the United Kingdom, and the breed's popularity steadily continues to grow.

Miss Paton, and her first litter was lost due to distemper except one pup, Anna from Rozavel, who grew up to be a well-trained working dog. Anna is believed to be the only Rottweiler left in England when the Second World War was ended.

Mrs. Gray imported three other dogs before the war—Asta von Norden, Arnold v.d. Eichener and Vefa

released, and was sent to the Air Force for use during the war.

The real beginning of the breed in England is marked by the end of the war, since the ten years prior to the war's ending did not amount to even a breeding pair of Rottweilers in England. Anna was the only bitch in the U.K., and by 1945 she was nine years old and hardly in breeding condition. She retired as a pet quite happily.

While serving in Germany as a veterinary officer, Captain Roy-Smith admired the Rottweiler,

Rottweiler enthusiasts strive to preserve the breed's best qualities.

Through importation of dogs from Germany, Holland and Sweden, and through careful breeding, the quality of Rottweilers in the U.K. steadily improved.

which he encountered many times while in the military. This young vet was the first to import a Rottweiler into the U.K. Although there are reports of Rottweilers in Britain as early as 1913, no dogs were registered with The Kennel Club when Captain Roy-Smith enquired. The Rottweilers that Roy-Smith imported as well as the foundation dogs imported by Mrs. Joanna Chadwick formed an important basis for the breed in Britain. These first Rottweilers came to England almost exclusively from Germany, and later from Holland and Sweden, where

the breed had established a stronghold. Among the British kennels that imported Rottweilers in the 1950s and '60s were: Rintelna, Mallion, Blackforest, Gamegards and Taucas.

The Rottweiler Club in the U.K. was established in 1960 by Mrs. M. Wait with an original membership of 25 Rottweiler fanciers, with Mrs. Gray serving as the first president, befitting her early efforts with the breed in the U.K. The second club, known as

the British Rottweiler Association, was also formed shortly thereafter, and the two clubs, surprisingly, cooperate well with one another.

Post-War Dogs Imported into England

Dog	Breeder	Date whelped	Importer
Berny v Weyher	Carl Voigt	June 11, 1952	Capt. Roy-Smith
Ajax v. Fuhrenkamp	Wilhelm Drevenstedt	April 20, 1952	Capt. Roy-Smith
Wuinta Eulenspiegel	Marieanne Bruns	February 28, 1954	Mrs. Joanna Chadwick
Rudi Eulenspiegel	Marieanne Bruns	May 21, 1954	Mrs. Joanna Chadwick
Rintelna Lotte v Osterberg	?	February 1952	Captain Roy-Smith
Bim Eulenspiegel	Marieanne Bruns	May 19, 1958	Mrs. Joanna Chadwick & Mr. Newton
Vera v Filstalstrand	?	?	Capt. Roy-Smith & Mary Macphail

By the late 1960s, the Rottweiler qualified for Challenge Certificates at championship shows of The Kennel Club. The first champion was made up in 1966, a bitch by the name of Chesara Dark Destiny, owned by Pat Lanz.

THE ROTTWEILER IN THE U.S.

The 1930s marked the first Rottweilers to be registered with the American Kennel Club, beginning with a German-bred bitch named Stina v Felsenmeer, owned by August Knecht. The first litter bred in the U.S. was accomplished by Otto Denny in September 1930. AKC recognition of the breed was achieved in 1931, with very few Rottweilers in the country and no standard accepted. Knecht and Denny mated their dogs to produce the first AKC-registered litter. Other litters were registered with AKC over the next couple of decades, mainly by German immigrants who had been Rottweiler breeders in the Fatherland.

The first AKC champion to earn that title in 1948, Zero was owned and bred by Noel P. Jones.

His litter sister Zola became the second champion, owned by Erna Pinkerton. Jones later handled Ch. Kurt to a Group One, the first Working Group to be claimed by a Rottweiler. The breed became more known as an obedience titleist than a conformation show champion, with Ch. Zada's Zenda, CD becoming the first Rottweiler to win an obedience title. Gero v Rabenhorst, an important import, qualified for CD, CDX and UD, the first three progressive titles in American obedience trials. This accomplishment in 1941 marked the first Rottweiler to reach the UD title.

Laura Coonley holds the distinction of the first person to breed an American Best in Show Rottweiler. The victorious dog was Ch. Kato v. Donnaj, CDX, TD, owned by Jan Marshall. Kato did not enjoy the distinction of the only BIS Rottweiler for very long, as his own brother Ch. Rodsden's Duke Du Trier swept the victory the very next day. It was May 1971. Duke

The Rottweiler in the U.S. initially was better known for its success in obedience competition rather than in the conformation ring.

While the Rottweiler is not as popular in the U.K. as it is in Germany, or the U.S. for that matter, it does have a strong, devoted following, led by breeders who have over a quarter-century's experience in the breed. Given the many positive qualities of the breed, its strength, impressive stature and biddable nature, the Rottweiler continues to gain new friends in the U.K. every year.

repeated his victory in Canada, becoming the first Rottweiler to win BIS in that country.

While the Rottweiler has had five important breed clubs in the U.S., the American Rottweiler Club, established in 1971, is the official parent club. Amongst the other clubs there are the Colonial Rottweiler Club, the Medallion Rottweiler Club and the Golden State Rottweiler Club. Each club is a separate entity, though each club stands for the betterment of the breed and the protection of the breed standard in the U.S.

Few breeds have excelled in the U.S. like the Rottweiler. The 1990s have been coloured in black and tan, and the Rottweiler has reigned as one of the nation's most popular breeds. Only out-registered by the Labrador Retriever, the Rottweiler rode out the 1990s with numbers exceeding hundreds of thousands of dogs. What is remarkable about this accomplishment is that the Rottweiler is a medium-large dog with no small amount of power and determination. As we will see, it is not a dog for everyone, yet many Americans seem to relate to its distinctive stature and proud strength, which accurately reflects its noble German ancestry.

This noble German breed has attracted many an admirer in the United States.

Why the Rottweiler?

Unlike the other breeds that have heralded top ranks in popularity, the Rottweiler is neither a sweet hunting dog (like the Labrador Retriever, Golden Retriever or Cocker Spaniel) nor an adoring shepherd type (like the German Shepherd Dog). Neither does he have any similarity to the Poodle, other than the affection of the German people for both breeds. No, the Rottweiler is a massive, hard-working dog whose weight can exceed 100 pounds (45 kgs) and whose height can be up to 27 inches (approx. 68 cms). Surely, the Rottweiler must possess many fine attributes to endear him to the likes of so many dog owners around the world.

The Rottweiler's strength and courage earned him favouritism early in the twentieth century. After suffering great neglect in the early 1900s, the breed was 'drafted' into service in World War I. The breed's performance for the Axis powers proved its superior abilities as a military dog, thus the Rottweiler's outstanding performance in Schutzhund decades later. Living in today's society, with a high crime rate in both cities and smaller towns, a guard dog with impressive size and ability to

The Rottweiler is as popular as a family pet as he is for guard and protection work.

Although considered a mastiff breed, the Rottweiler bears little resemblance to the Neapolitan Mastiff, shown here.

match is greatly in demand, as the registration statistics demonstrate year after year.

PHYSICAL CHARACTERISTICS

Unlike other mastiff breeds, such as the Neapolitan Mastiff, the Dogue de Bordeaux and the Bullmastiff, the Rottweiler is a handsome dog—balanced, well proportioned and not exaggerated like the aforementioned giants that suffer from acromegaly and worse conditions. It is even fair to say that for the Rottweiler's size, he is a very healthy dog, suffering only from hip dysplasia and a few other conditions, and his lifespan is greater than other dogs his size. The Rottweiler's sleek

When searching for a Rottweiler, owners are well advised to not seek out dogs that are bigger than the standard describes. These dogs will more likely suffer from joint problems and other conditions that accompany overbreeding and oversized dogs.

black coat, accented by its perfectly placed mahogany markings, cuts a handsome figure. His head is impressive but not so massive that it is out of proportion with his body. He is, by all counts, a majestic animal of considerable size, though he is not as giant as the Mastiff and the others.

PERSONALITY

A major attribute that the Rottweiler possesses in spades is its trainability. This is a most intelligent and obedient dog, capable of learning a multitude of tasks. His history as a droving dog, military and protection dog and obedience and show dog speaks well of the Rottweiler's diversity and versatility.

The Rottweiler is a naturally protective animal, with the strength to back up its protective instincts. Many trainers advise undertaking the Rottweiler's education with great caution, given the natural instincts and strength of this dog. Schutzhund training has been used with great success when executed by professional handlers in a controlled environment. Novices should not even consider attempting to sleeve train (i.e., attack train) the Rottweiler. Professional assistance is a must. In Germany there are countless experienced, expert Schutzhund trainers; in England and the U.S. it is more difficult to secure the services of such qualified professionals, and therefore extreme caution is advised when considering this type of training.

The Rottweiler is trustworthy and confident, befitting his stature and his proud German upbringing. There are stories about Rottweilers' being employed as 'moneyholders' for trade, with a money bag tied around the Rottweiler's

character of the breed: 'His figure, which is short, compact, and strong in proportion, gives every indication not only of high intelli-

Intelligence, pride and even temperament are all evident in the Rottweiler's expression.

gence but also of wonderful devotion, eagerness, and joy in work. A tractable dog with considerable power and stubborn endurance. His general appearance immedi-

Rottweilers are so popular because they are so versatile. They are family dogs, working dogs, guard dogs and tracking dogs.

neck. Trust and strength go paw in paw with the Rottweiler.

The German standard for the Rottweiler, as accepted by the ADRK, well describes the ideal

ately proclaims him to be of determination and courage; his calm glance indicates his good humour and his unswerving fidelity. His nature exhibits no traces of dis-

A Rottweiler will form a strong bond with his owner; fidelity and reliability are predominant characteristics of the breed.

quietude, hastiness or indecision. Treachery, maliciousness and falseness are entirely foreign to his nature.'

Certainly the German standard describes a dog that goes far to impress many dog lovers: the qualities of fidelity, good humour and decisiveness are welcome in a dog with the Rottweiler's size and power. The Rottweiler is at once friendly and imposing. He does not make friends without reservations: a stranger is a stranger, not like the retrievers who accept everyone immediately as a close friend. Rottweilers are discerning, as their

once owned a bitch that was extremely fond of my oldest son and had less devotion to the girls of our family. Nonetheless, the daughters of that bitch were affectionate and protective to all members of our family. Rottweilers tend to be individualistic—again, because they are smart and discerning creatures.

This intelligence does affect their trainability. As is commonly said of cats, they are too smart to proceed with constant repetition of a command. Once they have executed a command once or twice to your liking, they will likely tire of the 'game' and look for a better outlet. 'Why do humans persist in doing these silly procedures so many times? I got it the first time and it wasn't that exciting,' thinks the Rottweiler. Some Rottweilers need more prompting than others, and patience is required when training a dog, no matter the breed.

If you have children in your home and are considering a Rott-

DID YOU KNOW?
In Schutzhund trials, dogs are rated by performance and can earn the titles of SchH I (beginner), SchH II (intermediate) and SchH III (master). These titles can be appended to the dog's name and pedigree.

intelligence and good judgement allow. Their protective nature underscores this judgement as well, but once a Rottweiler has accepted you as a friend, you can be sure that you have a buddy to rely upon.

Rottweilers are ideal as protectors of family and property. The breed accepts each member of the family and is equally protective of father as he is of the smallest child. Rottweilers do not usually play favourites, though there are exceptions to every rule. We

weiler, there are matters to be considered. A well-bred Rottweiler reared in a family with love and fairness is as trustworthy with children as the best of dogs. Given the Rottweiler's size and strength, however, many parents may choose not to take a chance. This is every parent's prerogative, but accidents and dog bites can happen with any breed. Actually there are far more instances of Cocker Spaniels biting children than any breed, including Rottweilers and Pit Bull Terriers. Any dog can do harm with its bite, regardless of size, and larger dogs tend to bite less intensely since they are confident about their strength. If you know the breeder of your dog and have discussed the temperament of dogs in that line, you should have faith in the Rottweiler that you purchase. Of course, caution is the rule, and you must never allow the Rottweiler to get the upper hand, whether the dog is dealing with the biggest man in

the house or the smallest toddler. Dogs like to have positive examples to follow or else they try to become leaders. Their pack

The pet Rottweiler will love and protect all members of the family.

instinct enforces their need to have a leader—that leader must be you, followed by each member of your family. The Rottweiler must understand that he has the lowest rank in the household.

Are you well suited, indeed worthy, to own a Rottweiler? Have you the physical stamina to keep up with such a dog? Have you a fenced garden to provide ample exercise? Do you have the time to give a dog whose dedication and protectiveness are centred around you?

Not everyone is fit to own a Rottweiler. That much is obvious. You must not be hasty in deciding that this dog is for you and your home and family. Every dog deserves a fair shot and the best possible living situation possible. The Rottweiler needs a confident, competent owner who understands his needs and is able to provide properly for him.

Schutzhund, carting, herding tests, backpacking and camping, therapy (PAT) visits, public

A well-trained Rottweiler will accept children and other pets and still be protective against strangers and intruders.

27

Rottweilers should have well-formed teeth. Brushing and regular dental exams will keep them that way for the life of the dog.

demonstrations and more. Your time with your Rottweiler is only limited by your imagination, time and budget. Certainly your Rottweiler is the kind of dog who likes to try anything once. Since the breed has such a high level of trust for its human counterparts, Rottweilers will follow their owners to the ends of the earth!

HEALTH CONSIDERATIONS FOR THE ROTTWEILER

Our Rottweilers are generally healthy, active dogs. Advances in veterinary medicine, just as in human medicine, result in increased life spans, but in our pets this has not proven to be a

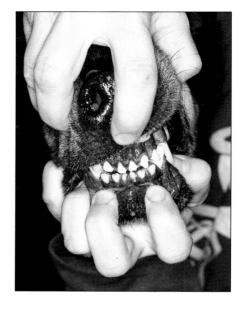

Given the many talents of the Rottweiler, as its history as a drover dog, protection dog, military dog, etc., has conveyed, you must find outlets for your Rottweiler's abilities. You cannot leave your Rottweiler alone in the garden for eight hours without supervision or, worse, tied to a post to run in circles of boredom until you decide to check on him. No, Rottweilers are creative, intelligent creatures that need activities. Whether it is a run on the beach every evening, a jog through the park in the morning, or a full-blown itinerary of challenging events, your Rottweiler will be grateful. Some of the kinds of events that inventive Rottweiler owners enjoy with their dogs include obedience trials, agility trials, tracking, herding tests and more.

reliable hypothesis. Rottweilers reach their senior years at around seven years old, which seems considerably young to us humans who do not retire until 55 or 65! In order to ensure our Rottweilers the longest possible life, and the healthiest one, we must be informed and provide our pets with the best health care possible.

This begins, of course, with visits to the vet and a proper schedule of vaccinations. Back in the late 1970s, a fatal disease known as parvovirus was first recorded. While it is a manageable disease today, without proper vaccinations, early diagnosis and prompt treatment, it can be deadly. Many prominent breeders throughout the 1980s and '90s lost valuable puppies to this dreaded disease. Your veterinary surgeon will inform you of the best inoculation schedule, which usually begins at around eight weeks of age and is repeated every few weeks until around four months, and then followed up every six months until two years. Research has indicated that Rottweilers' immune systems are weaker than those of other breeds, so absolute care is required to protect the breed from parvovirus, to which it seems unfortunately very susceptible.

As with most large breeds of dog, hip and elbow dysplasia have taken their toll on the Rottweiler breed. Hip dysplasia, first recognised as a major problem in German Shepherd Dogs, has crippled (or badly deformed) many Rottweilers. Hip dysplasia in its severest form can render a dog totally crippled. Since it is a

hereditary condition, no Rottweiler who tests positive for hip dysplasia should be bred. While the incidence of hip dysplasia has been reduced since the 1970s when it was around 30 percent, today approximately 20 percent of Rottweilers test positive for the disease. Still worse, the incidence of elbow dysplasia in Rottweilers is upsettingly high, with the percentage around 40 to 50 percent, and higher in males than females. Responsible breeders must test for both forms of dysplasia before breeding their dogs. Years ago, certain dysplastic champions were still extensively bred and therefore the number of puppies born with dysplasia was disturbingly high. Today, breeders exclude such dogs from their programmes, regardless of their positive conformational value.

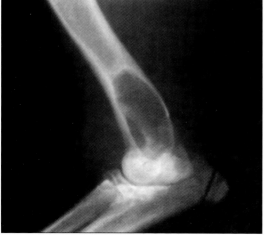
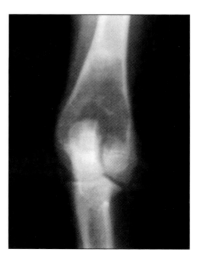

Elbow dysplasia in a three-and-a-half-year-old dog.

Discuss hip dysplasia and elbow dysplasia with your breeder. This is your best way to determine how cognisant of the problem the breeder is. A number of breeders propose that environmental factors also affect dysplasia in Rottweilers. Breeders who do not use non-slip matting in their whelping boxes may aggravate the potential condition. As puppies try to take their first steps and begin to slide around on the hard slippery surface of the whelping pen, their fragile ligaments and bones can be badly stressed. Since both types of dysplasia occur when the Rottweiler is fairly young (before 24 months for HD, before 7 months for ED), such a theory is believable. Other breeders propose that the diet of the puppy can affect the development of dysplasia and other cartilage diseases like osteochondrosis in susceptible dogs. Diets that are high in calcium, protein and fats should be discouraged, since Rottweilers are fast growing dogs with the potential of putting too much weight too fast on their growing frames. Let's not rule out exercise from the picture—young Rottweilers should not be permitted to roughhouse and jump about wildly in play, since such unregulated exercise can result in cartilage tears and other injuries that may increase the risk of problems with osteochondrosis, HD or ED.

DO YOU KNOW ABOUT HIP DYSPLASIA?

Hip dysplasia is a fairly common condition found in Rottweilers, as well as other large breeds. When a dog has hip dysplasia, its hind leg has an incorrectly formed hip joint. By constant use of the hip joint, it becomes more and more loose, wears abnormally and may become arthritic.

Hip dysplasia can only be confirmed with an X-ray, but certain symptoms may indicate a problem. Your Rottweiler may have a hip dysplasia problem if it walks in a peculiar manner, hops instead of smoothly running, uses its hind legs in unison (to keep the pressure off the weak joint), has trouble getting up from a prone position and sits with both legs together on one side of its body.

As the dog matures, it may adapt well to life with a bad hip, but in a few years the arthritis develops and many Rottweilers with hip dysplasia become cripples.

Hip dysplasia is considered an inherited disease and can usually be diagnosed when the dog is three to nine months old. Some experts claim that a special diet might help your puppy outgrow the bad hip, but the usual treatments are surgical—the removal of the pectineus muscle, the removal of the round part of the femur, reconstructing the pelvis and replacing the hip with an artificial one. All of these surgical interventions are expensive, but they are usually very successful. Follow the advice of your veterinary surgeon.

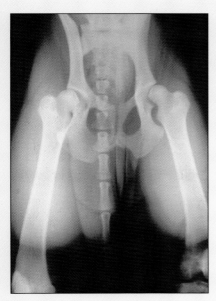

Compare the two hip joints and you'll understand dysplasia. Hip dysplasia is a badly worn hip joint caused by improper fit of the bone into the socket. It is easily the most common hip problem in Rottweilers.

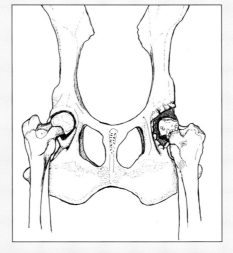

The healthy hip joint on the left and the unhealthy hip joint on the right.

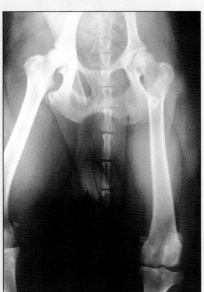

Hip dysplasia can only be positively diagnosed by x-ray. Rottweilers manifest the problem when they are between three and nine months of age, the so-called fast growth period.

The deep-chested Rottweiler is prone to bloat, especially if vigorous exercise follows mealtime too closely.

Another problem that is related to Rottweilers is known as bloat, sometimes referred to by vets as gastric volvulus or gastric dilatation. Deep-chested, large dogs are the most susceptible to this condition, characterised by the stomach's being distended with air, which is swallowed by the dog. Generally this is not a problem with puppies but with adults or older dogs. Dogs who tend to wolf their food and water, who run and play very vigorously or who are stressed by other factors are candidates for bloat. In the worst-case scenario, a dog whose stomach has bloated will die

The behaviour and personality of your Rottweiler will reflect your care and training more than any breed characteristics or indications. Remember that these dogs require a purposeful existence and plan your relationship around activities that serve this most basic and important need. All the good potential of the breed will necessarily follow.

from the stomach's twisting, which stops the flow of food to the organ as well as the blood supply. Unfortunately, about one-third of the dogs who suffer from this condition will die, though immediate veterinary assistance can prevent death.

Many vets and breeders make recommendations to Rottweiler owners to help prevent the possible onset of bloat.

Since Rottweilers tend to love mealtime, their excitement can result in their gulping or wolfing their food. You want to discourage this as much as possible. Feed smaller meals two or three times a day. You can try placing large balls or chew toys in the bowl so that your dog has to eat around them. Always serve dry food that has been saturated in water. Use bowl stands to elevate the dog's food. Take away the dog's fresh water at meal times, but leave it available throughout the day. Do not leave your dog's food sitting around all day. Place it down only at the designated meal times, and pick

You want your Rottweiler to stay healthy and active; practise preventative medicine and be proactive in his care.

it up as soon as the dog walks away from the bowl. Schedule exercise times so that there is at least 90 minutes before and after each meal. These simple suggestions can mean the difference between life and death for your black-and-tan friend. It is but a small price to pay for all your Rottweiler gives you in terms of companionship, protection and amusement!

Other conditions that you may want to discuss with your vet include hypothyroidism, the most frequently seen hormonal condition in Rottweilers; osteochondrosis, a condition seen in young dogs that affects the cartilage; aortic stenosis, a congenital defect of the heart; degenerative myelopathy, affecting the spinal cord; progressive retinal atrophy and retinal dysplasia, congenital disorders of the retina that can result in blindness; and von Willebrand's disease, the most common congenital disease of the blood affecting the clotting factor.

While this list may seem daunting to the Rottweiler enthusiast, we present it here not to discourage your interest in our great breed, but instead to promote your responsible husbandry of these truly worthy animals. Surely the list of diseases seen in humans would be as disheartening! Be a responsible owner, be informed and enjoy the longest possible life with your Rottweiler.

33

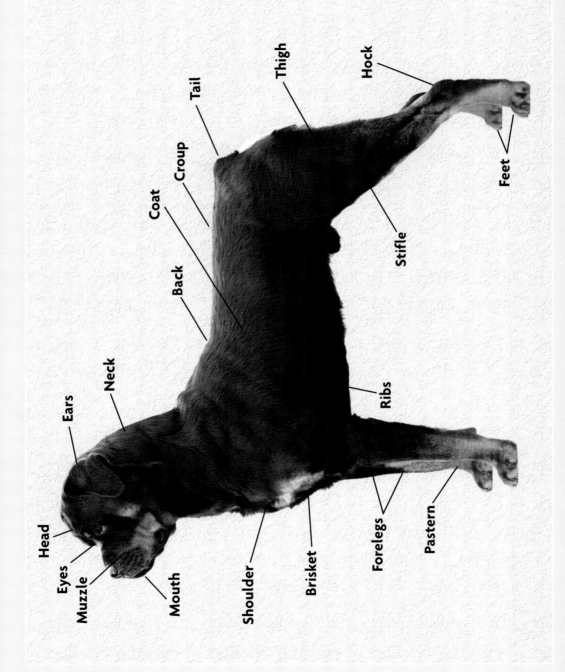

Thigh

Hock

Tail

Croup

Feet

Coat

Stifle

Back

Neck

Ears

Ribs

Head

Eyes

Muzzle

Mouth

Shoulder

Brisket

Forelegs

Pastern

Breed Standard
for the Rottweiler

Each breed of purebred dog has an accepted breed standard, a written description of what breeders and judges agree is the perfect dog; in this case, the perfect Rottweiler. Each national breed club—the ADRK in Germany, the American Rottweiler Club in the U.S., etc., draws up a standard and it is submitted to the national kennel club (The German Kennel Club, The Kennel Club, The American Kennel Club, etc). Once the national club accepts the standard, the breed is 'recognised' and the standard becomes the guide for the fancy to evaluate the quality of an individual animal. Of course, no dog can be completely perfect according to the standard, but breeders continually try to breed closer and closer to that perfect Rottweiler.

From country to country, breed standards vary considerably in word-

Though breeders strive for perfection in their dogs, and some come close, there is no such thing as a 'perfect' Rottweiler.

Head and Skull: Head medium length, skull broad between ears. Forehead moderately arched as seen from side. Occipital bone well developed but not conspicuous. Cheeks well boned and muscled but not prominent. Skin on head not loose, although it may form a moderate wrinkle when attentive. Muzzle fairly deep with topline level, and length of muzzle in relation to distance from well defined stop to occiput to be as 2 to 3. Nose well developed with proportionately large nostrils, always black.

Eyes: Medium size, almond-shaped, dark brown in colour, light eye undesirable, eyelids close fitting.

Ears: Pendant, small in proportion rather than large, set high and wide apart, lying flat and close to cheek.

You may want to have a breeder evaluate your Rottweiler's conformation before deciding to show your dog.

ing, interpretation, content and the like. The Rottweiler, however, is fairly uniform from country to country, unlike some breeds such as the German Shepherd Dog and Shetland Sheepdog.

THE KENNEL CLUB STANDARD FOR THE ROTTWEILER

General Appearance: Above average size, stalwart dog. Correctly proportioned, compact and powerful form, permitting great strength, manoeuvrability and endurance.

Head skin should not be loose, though a modest wrinkle when the dog is attentive is acceptable.

Characteristics: Appearance displays boldness and courage. Self-assured and fearless. Calm gaze should indicate good humour.

Temperament: Good natured, not nervous, aggressive or vicious; courageous, biddable, with natural guarding instincts.

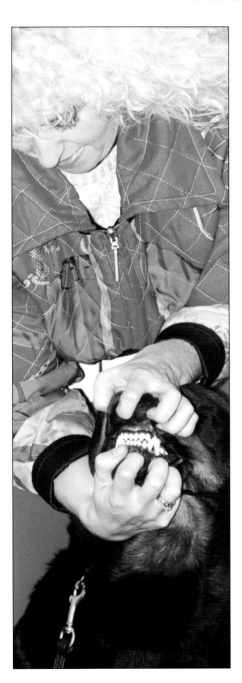

Mouth: Teeth strong, complete dentition with scissor bite, i.e. upper teeth closely overlapping lower teeth and set square to the jaws. Flews black and firm, falling gradually away towards corners of mouth, which do not protrude excessively.

Neck: Of fair length, strong, round and very muscular. Slightly arched, free from throatiness.

Forequarters: Shoulders well laid back, long and sloping, elbows well let down, but not loose. Legs straight, muscular, with plenty of bone and substance. Pasterns sloping slightly forward.

Body: Chest roomy, broad and deep with well sprung ribs. Depth of brisket will not be more, and not much less than 50 per cent of shoulder height. Back straight, strong and not too long, ratio of shoulder height to length of body should be as 9 is to 10, loins short, strong and deep, flanks not tucked up. Croup of proportionate length, and broad, very slightly sloping.

Hindquarters: Upper thigh not too short, broad and strongly muscled. Lower thigh well muscled at top, strong and sinewy below. Stifles fairly well bent. Hocks well angulated without exaggeration, metatarsals not completely vertical. Strength and soundness of hock highly desirable.

Feet: Strong, round and compact with toes well arched. Hindfeet somewhat

Rottweilers are required to have a scissor bite. The upper teeth should slightly overlap the lower teeth.

37

Well-bred Rottweilers should have the required markings, as defined by the standard, both in front and in back.

The Rottweiler's coat consists of a top coat and an undercoat.

longer than front. Pads very hard, toenails short, dark and strong. Rear dewclaws removed.

Tail: Normally carried horizontally, but slightly above horizontal when dog is alert. Customarily docked at first joint, it is strong and not set too low.

Gait/Movement: Conveys an impression of supple strength, endurance and purpose. While back remains firm and stable there is a powerful hindthrust and good stride. First and foremost, movement should be harmonious, positive and unrestricted.

Coat: Consists of top coat and undercoat. Top coat is of medium length, coarse and flat. Undercoat, essential on the neck and thighs, should not show through top coat. Hair may also be a little longer on the back of the forelegs and breechings. Long or excessively wavy coat highly undesirable.

Colour: Black with clearly defined markings as follows: a spot over each eye, on cheeks, as a strip around each side of muzzle, but not on bridge of nose, on throat, two clear triangles on either side of the breast bone, on forelegs from carpus downward to toes, on inside of rear legs from hock to toes, but not completely eliminating black from back of legs, under tail. Colour of markings from rich tan to mahogany and should not exceed 10 per cent of body colour. White marking is highly undesirable. Black pencil markings on toes are desirable. Undercoat is grey, fawn, or black.

Size: Dogs height at shoulder: between 63–69 cms (25–27 ins); bitches between 58–63.5 cms (23–25 ins). Height should always be considered in relation to general appearance.

Faults: Any departure from the foregoing points should be considered a fault and the seriousness with which the fault should be regarded should be in exact proportion to its degree.

Note: Male animals should have two apparently normal testicles fully descended into the scrotum.

	CORRECT	**INCORRECT**

EARS
Skull should be broad between ears; ears should lie flat and close to cheek.

FOREQUARTERS
Chest should be roomy and broad; legs should be straight and should look strong and muscular.

HINDQUARTERS
Legs should be strong, with musculature apparent in both upper and lower thigh, and no exaggeration.

BACK
Should be straight and strong, and should appear stable both in motion and at rest. Should not have a roach back (1) or sway back (2).

1

2

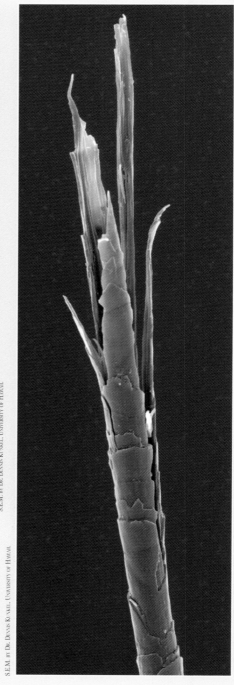

Rottweiler hairs greatly magnified. The S.E.M. above shows a hair in poor condition, as evidenced by the lack of uniformity of the cuticle. The hair to the right shows split ends. The facing page shows healthy top coat and undercoat hairs.

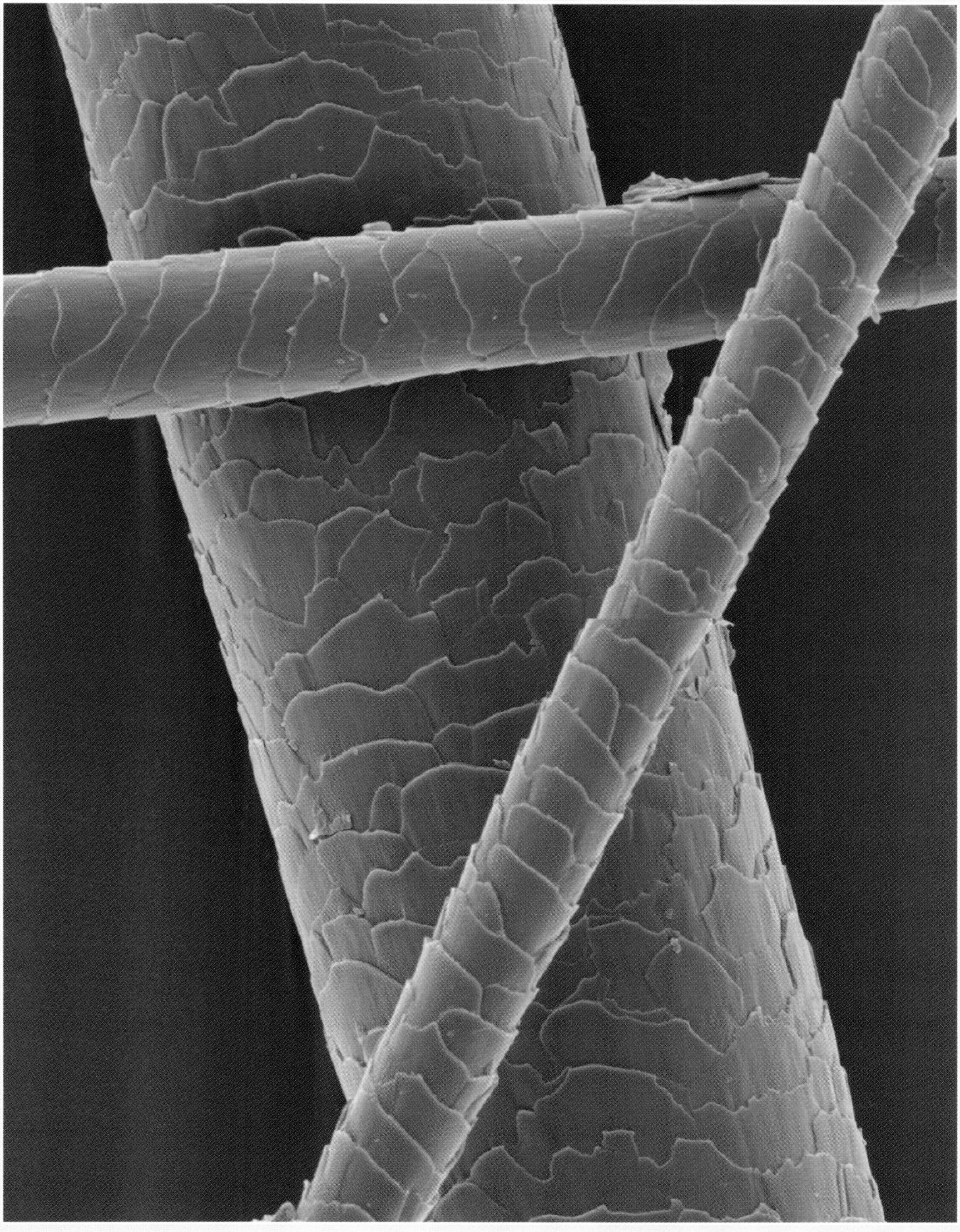

S.E.M. by Dr. Dennis Kunkel, University of Hawaii.

Your Rottweiler Puppy

ARE YOU A ROTTWEILER PERSON?

Owning a Rottweiler puppy is similar to raising a child. Puppies are just as demanding as children...but puppyhood is a lot shorter than childhood.

Have you ever been to the home of a friend or relative who owned a large, unruly dog? This untrained, attention-starved creature hurls itself at company, climbing upon your lap, mounting your leg, and the like... Of course, the owner does not seem to notice, and has no means to discipline or control the animal. A nuisance, at least; a crime, maybe! You must make a very difficult choice here. Do you really want the responsibility of owning and training a Rottweiler? He is a demanding animal. He is also very smart and needs your total concentration. A primary consideration is time, not only the time of the animal's allotted life span, which can be eight to ten years or more, but also the time required for the

owner to exercise and care for the creature. If you are not committed to the welfare and whole existence of this energetic, purposeful animal; if, in the simplest, most basic example, you are not willing to walk

your dog daily, despite the weather, do not choose a Rottweiler as a companion.

Space is another important consideration. The Rottweiler in early puppyhood may be well accommodated in a corner of your kitchen but after only six months, when the dog is likely over 60 or 70 pounds, larger space certainly will be required. A

Your puppy should have a well-fed appearance but not a distended abdomen, which may indicate worms or incorrect feeding, or both. The body should be firm, with a solid feel. The skin of the abdomen should be pale pink and clean, without signs of scratching or rash. Check the hind legs to make certain that dewclaws were removed, if any were present at birth.

42

garden with a fence is also a basic and reasonable expectation.

In addition, there are the usual problems associated with puppies of any breed like the damages likely to be sustained by your floors, furniture, flowers and, not least of all, to your freedom (of movement), as in holiday or weekend trips. This union is a serious affair and should be deeply considered, but once decided, your choice of a Rottweiler can be the most rewarding of all breeds. A few suggestions will help in the purchase of your dog.

PURCHASING THE ROTTWEILER PUPPY

Most likely you are seeking a pet Rottweiler, not necessarily a show dog. That does not mean that you are looking for a second-rate model. A 'pet-quality' Rottweiler is not like a second-hand car or a 'slightly irregular' suit jacket. Your pet must be as sound, healthy and temperamentally fit as any top show dog. Pet owners do not want a Rottweiler who can't run smoothly and easily, who is not trustworthy and reliable around children and strangers, who does not look like a Rottweiler. You are not buying a black-and-tan hound dog, you want a Rottweiler— a handsome guard dog with a nice expression and head, sound hips, good eyes and a loveable personality. If these qualities are not important to you as a Rottweiler owner, then you should go to the shelter and rescue a homeless mutt!

The safest method of obtaining your new Rottweiler puppy is to seek out a local reputable breeder.

Unless you want to enter dog shows, you don't need a show dog. Get a pet-quality Rottweiler from a reputable breeder.

This is suggested even if you are not looking for a show specimen. The novice breeders and pet owners who advertise at attractive prices in

Two important documents you will get from the breeder are the pup's pedigree and registration papers. The breeder should register the litter and each pup with The Kennel Club, and it is necessary for you to have the paperwork if you plan on showing or breeding in the future.

Make sure you know the breeder's intentions on which type of registration he will obtain for the pup. There are limited registrations which may prohibit the dog from being shown or from competing in non-conformation trials such as Working or Agility if the breeder feels that the pup is not of sufficient quality to do so. There is also a type of registration that will permit the dog in non-conformation competition only.

If your dog is registered with a Kennel-Club-recognised breed club, then you can register the pup with The Kennel Club yourself. Your breeder can assist you with the specifics of the registration process.

The puppy leaves for his new home! Be sure to ask about inoculations, de-worming and the name and address of the vet who cared for the dam and her litter.

the local newspapers are probably kind enough towards their dogs, but perhaps do not have the expertise or facilities required to successfully raise these animals. These pet puppies are frequently badly weaned and left with the mother too long without the supplemental feeding required by this fast-growing breed. This lack of proper feeding can cause indigestion, rickets, weak bones, poor teeth and other problems. Veterinary bills may soon distort initial savings into financial, or worse, emotional loss.

Inquire about inoculations and when the puppy was last dosed for worms. Check the ears for any signs of mites or irritation. Are the eyes clear and free of any debris? The puppy coat is softer than the adult coat, but the coat should still be jet black and the tan markings should be visible, if not as pronounced as on the dam. Your puppy should have a dark nose and, preferably, dark toenails. This

is a consideration of pigmentation, which should not be confused with colour. It is wise to choose a puppy with deep rich pigmentation and as much black as possible. Deep eyes are best in any colour. Look for expression in your puppy's eyes, as this is a good sign of intelligence.

Note the way your choice moves. The Rottweiler, even in puppyhood, should show sound, deliberate movement with no tendency to stumble or drag the hind feet. Do not mistake a little puppy awkwardness for a physical defect. Rottweiler puppies often are not skilled at coordinating their big paws perfectly just yet. Look at the mouth to make sure that the bite is fairly even, although maturity can often correct errors present at puppyhood. If you have any doubts, ask to see the parents' mouths. This brings up an important point—do not purchase a puppy without first seeing at least one of the parents.

Another important consideration remains to be discussed and that is the sex of your puppy. For a family companion, a Rottweiler bitch is the better choice, considering the female's inbred concern for all young creatures and her accompanying tolerance and patience. If you do not intend to spay your pet when she has matured or is well over her growing period, then extra care is required during the times of her heat.

COMMITMENT OF OWNERSHIP

After considering all of these factors, you have most likely already made some very important decisions about selecting your puppy. You have chosen a Rottweiler, which means that you have decided which characteristics you want in a dog and what type of dog will best fit into your family and lifestyle. If you have selected a breeder, you have gone a step further—you have done your research and found a responsible, conscientious person who breeds quality Rottweilers and who should be a

reliable source of help as you and your puppy adjust to life together. If you have observed a litter in action, you have obtained a first-hand look at the dynamics of a puppy 'pack' and, thus, you have gotten to learn about each pup's individual personality—perhaps you have even found one that particularly appeals to you.

A small puppy is a big responsibility.

However, even if you have not yet found the Rottweiler puppy of your dreams, observing pups will help you learn to recognise certain behaviour and to determine what a pup's behaviour indicates about his temperament. You will be able to pick out which pups are the leaders, which ones are less outgoing, which ones are confident, which ones are shy, playful, friendly, aggressive, etc. Equally as important, you will learn to recognise what a healthy pup should look and act like. All of these things will help you in your search, and when you find the Rottweiler that was meant for you, you will know it!

He's all yours... including the responsibility to feed, care and educate him. Are you ready for that?

The cost of food must also be mentioned. This is not a breed that can be maintained on table scraps and light supplement. Rottweilers need a good supply of protein to develop the bone and muscle required in a working animal. Rottweilers are not picky eaters but unless fed properly they can quickly succumb to skin problems.

Unfortunately, when a puppy is purchased by someone who does not take into consideration the time and attention that dog ownership requires, it is the puppy who suffers when he is either abandoned or placed in a shelter by a frustrated owner. So all of the 'homework' you do in preparation for your pup's arrival will benefit you both. The more informed you are, the more you will know what to expect and the better equipped you will be to handle the ups and downs of raising a puppy. Hopefully, everyone in the household is willing to do his part in raising and caring for the pup. The anticipation of owning a dog often brings a lot of promises from excited family members: 'I will walk him every day,' 'I will feed him,' 'I will housebreak him,' etc., but these things take time and effort, and promises can easily be forgotten once the novelty of the new pet has worn off.

Researching your breed, selecting a responsible breeder and observing as many pups as possible

Caring for the dog should be shared by all family members.

are all important steps on the way to dog ownership. It may seem like a lot of effort...and you have not

even brought the pup home yet! Remember, though, you cannot be too careful when it comes to deciding on the type of dog you want and finding out about your prospective pup's background. Buying a puppy is not—or should not be—just another whimsical purchase. In fact, this is one instance in which you actually *do* get to choose your own family! But, you may be thinking, buying a puppy should be fun—it should not be so serious and so much work. If you keep in mind the thought that your puppy is not a cuddly stuffed toy or decorative lawn ornament, but instead will become a real member of your family, you will realise that while buying a puppy is a pleasurable and exciting endeavour, it is not something to be taken lightly. Relax...the fun will start when the pup comes home!

Always keep in mind that a puppy is nothing more than a baby in a furry disguise...a baby who is virtually helpless in a human world and who trusts his owner for fulfilment of his basic needs for survival. That goes beyond food, water and shelter; your pup needs care, protection, guidance and love. If you are not prepared to commit to this, then you are not prepared to own a dog.

Wait a minute, you say. How hard could this be? All of my neighbours own dogs and they seem to be doing just fine. Why should I have to worry about all of this? Well, you *should not* worry about it; in fact, you will probably find that once

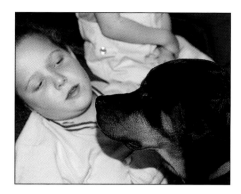

cific area in the house, or will he be allowed to roam as he pleases? Will he spend most of his time in the house or will he be primarily an outdoor dog? Whatever you decide, you must ensure that he has a place that he can 'call his own.'

When you bring your new puppy into your home, you are bringing him into what will become his home as well. Obviously, you did not buy a puppy so that he could take over your house, but in order for a puppy to grow into a stable, well-adjusted dog, he has to feel comfortable in his surroundings. Remember, he is leaving the warmth and security of his mother and littermates, plus the familiarity

your Rottweiler pup gets used to his new home, he will fall into his place in the family quite naturally. But it never hurts to emphasise the commitment of dog ownership. With some time and patience, it is really not too difficult to raise a curious and exuberant Rottweiler pup to be a well-adjusted and well-mannered adult dog—a dog that could be your most loyal friend.

PREPARING PUPPY'S PLACE IN YOUR HOME

Researching your breed and finding a breeder are only two aspects of the 'homework' you will have to do before bringing your Rottweiler puppy home. You will also have to prepare your home and family for the new addition. Much like you would prepare a nursery for a newborn baby, you will need to designate a place in your home that will be the puppy's own. How you prepare your home will depend on how much freedom the dog will be allowed: will he be confined to one room or a spe-

Grooming tools, collars, leashes, dog beds and, of course, toys will be an expense to you when you first obtain your pup, and the cost will trickle on throughout your dog's lifetime. If your puppy damages or destroys your possessions (as most puppies surely will!) or something belonging to a neighbour, you can calculate additional expense. You can count on spending for flea and pest control, which every dog owner faces more than once. Also be sure to include dog food and treats along with routine vaccine inoculations and other veterinary expenses when considering the cost of caring for your pet. You must be able to handle the financial responsibility of owning a dog.

of the only place he has ever known, so it is important to make his transition as easy as possible. By preparing a place in your home for the puppy, you are making him feel as welcome as possible in a strange new place. It should not take him long to get used to it, but the sud-

Crates are a dog's best friend (besides you, of course!).

den shock of being transplanted is somewhat traumatic for a young pup. Imagine how a small child would feel in the same situation—that is how your puppy must be feeling. It is up to you to reassure him and to let him know, 'Little fellow, you are going to like it here!'

WHAT YOU SHOULD BUY
CRATE
To someone unfamiliar with the use of crates in dog training, it may seem like punishment to shut a dog in a crate; this is not the case at all. Crates are not cruel—crates have many humane and highly effective uses in dog care and training. For example, crate training is a very popular and very successful housebreaking method; a crate can keep your dog safe during travel; and, perhaps most importantly, a crate provides your dog with a place of his own in your home. It serves as a

Your local pet shop will have the crate best suited for your Rottweiler. Get the largest size suitable; while a small crate is satisfactory for your puppy, it won't be large enough when the dog matures.

'doggie bedroom' of sorts—your Rottweiler can curl up in his crate when he wants to sleep or when he just needs a break. Many dogs sleep in their crates overnight. When lined with soft blankets and with a favourite toy, a crate becomes a cosy pseudo-den for your dog. Like his ancestors, he too will seek out the comfort and retreat of a den—you just happen to be providing him with something a little more luxurious than leaves and twigs lining a dirty ditch.

As far as purchasing a crate, the type that you buy is up to you. It will most likely be one of the two

most popular types: wire or fibreglass. There are advantages and disadvantages to each type. For example, a wire crate is more open, allowing the air to flow through and affording the dog a view of what is going on around him. A fibreglass crate, however, is sturdier and can double as a travel crate since it provides more protection for the dog. The size of the crate is another

that the pup would use in the wild to make a den; the pup can make his own 'burrow' in the crate. Although your pup is far removed from his den-making ancestors, the denning instinct is still a part of his genetic makeup. Second, until you bring your pup home, he has been sleeping amidst the warmth of his mother and littermates, and while a blanket is not the same as a warm, breathing body, it still provides heat and something with which to snuggle. You will want to wash your pup's blankets frequently in case he has an accident in his crate, and replace or remove any blanket that becomes ragged and starts to fall apart.

Be prepared for your pup's arrival. Ask your veterinary surgeon to recommend the equipment you will need.

thing to consider. Puppies do not stay puppies forever—in fact, sometimes it seems as if they grow right before your eyes. A Yorkie-sized crate may be fine for a very young Rottweiler pup, but it will not do him much good for long! Unless you have the money and the inclination to buy a new crate every time your pup has a growth spurt, it is better to get one that will accommodate your dog both as a pup and at full size. A large crate will be necessary for a full-grown Rottweiler, as their approximate weight range is between 75 and 110 pounds.

BEDDING
Veterinary bedding in the dog's crate will help the dog feel more at home. First, the bedding will take the place of the leaves, twigs, etc.,

During crate training, you should partition off the section of the crate in which the pup stays. If he is given too big of an area, this will hinder your training efforts. Crate training is based on the fact that a dog does not like to soil his sleeping quarters, so it is ineffective to keep a pup in a crate that is so big that he can eliminate in one end and get far enough away from it to sleep. Also, you want to make the crate den-like for the pup. Blankets and a toy will make the crate cosy for the small Rottweiler; as he grows, you may want to remove some of his blankets to make more room.

It will take some coaxing at first, but be patient. Given some time to get used to it, your pup will adapt to his new home-within-a-home quite nicely.

With a big variety of dog toys available, and so many that look like they would be a lot of fun for a dog, be careful in your selection. It is amazing what a set of puppy teeth can do to an innocent-looking toy, so, obviously, safety is a major consideration. Be sure to choose the most durable products that you can find. This is an especially important consideration with a breed like the Rottweiler who has naturally strong teeth and jaws. Hard nylon bones and toys are a safe bet, and many of them are offered in different scents and flavours that will be sure to capture your Rottweiler's attention. It is always fun to play a game of catch with your dog, and there are balls and flying discs that are specially made to withstand dog teeth.

Toys

Toys are a must for dogs of all ages, especially for curious playful pups. Puppies are the 'children' of the dog world, and what child does not love toys? Chew toys provide enjoyment to both dog and owner—your dog will enjoy playing with his favourite toys, while you will enjoy the fact that they distract him from your expensive shoes and leather sofa. Puppies love to chew; in fact, chewing is a physical need for pups as they are teething, and everything looks appetising! The full range of your possessions—from old dishrag to Oriental rug—is fair game in the eyes of a teething pup. Puppies are not all that discerning when it

Rottweiler puppies need to chew. Get your pup a HIGH-QUALITY durable chew device.

comes to finding something to literally 'sink their teeth into'—everything tastes great!

Stuffed toys are another option; these are good to put in the dog's crate to give him some company. Be careful of these, as a pup can de-stuff one pretty quickly, and stay away from stuffed toys with small plastic eyes or parts that a pup could choke on. Similarly, squeaky toys are quite popular. There are dogs that will come running from anywhere in the house at the first sound from their favourite squeaky friend. Again, if a pup de-stuffs one of these, the small plastic squeaker inside can be dangerous if swallowed. Monitor the condition of your pup's toys carefully and get rid of any that have been chewed to the point of becoming potentially dangerous.

Be careful of natural bones, which have a tendency to splinter into sharp, dangerous pieces. Also be careful of rawhide, which after enough chewing can turn into pieces that are easy to swallow, and also watch out for the mushy mess it can turn into on your carpet.

LEAD

A nylon lead is probably the best option as it is the most resistant to puppy teeth should your pup take a liking to chewing on his lead. Of course, this is a habit that should be nipped in the bud, but if your pup likes to chew on his lead he has a very slim chance of being able to chew through the strong nylon. Nylon leads are also lightweight, which is good for a young Rottweiler who is just getting used to the idea of walking on a lead. For everyday walking and safety purposes, the nylon lead is a good choice. As your pup grows up and gets used to walking on the lead, and can do it politely, you may want to purchase a flexible lead, which allows you either to extend the length to give the dog a broader area to explore or to pull in the lead when you want to keep him close. Of course there are special leads for training purposes, and specially made leather harnesses for the working Rottweiler, but these are not necessary for routine walks. If your Rottweiler is especially strong or tends to pull on the lead, you may want to purchase something stronger, like a thicker leather lead.

COLLAR

Your pup should get used to wearing a collar all the time since you will want to attach his ID tags to his collar. Also, the lead and collar go hand in hand—you have to attach the lead to something! A lightweight nylon collar will be a good choice; make sure that it fits snugly enough so that the pup cannot wriggle out of it, but loose enough so that it will not be uncomfortably tight around the pup's neck. You should be able to fit a finger in between the pup and the collar. It may take some time for your pup to

You will probably start feeding your Rottweiler pup the same food that he has been getting from the breeder; the breeder should give you a few days' supply to start you off. Although you should not give your pup too many treats, you will want to have puppy treats on hand for coaxing, training, rewards, etc. Be careful, though, as a small pup's calorie requirements are relatively low and a few treats can add up to almost a full day's worth of calories without the required nutrition.

get used to wearing the collar, but soon he will not even notice that it is there. Choke collars are made for training, but should only be used by an owner who knows exactly how to use it. If you use a stronger leather lead or a chain lead to walk your Rottweiler, you will need a stronger collar as well.

FOOD AND WATER BOWLS

Your pup will need two bowls, one for food and one for water. You may

He's lonesome! Your Rottweiler pup needs loving care to help him adjust to his new home.

because he does not know any better. All you can do is clean up any 'accidents'—old rags, towels, newspapers and a safe disinfectant are good to have on hand.

BEYOND THE BASICS

The items previously discussed are the bare necessities. You will find out what else you need as you go along—grooming supplies, flea/tick protection, baby gates to partition a room, etc.—these things will vary depending on your situation. It is just important that right away you have everything you need to feed and make your Rottweiler comfortable in his first few days at home.

want two sets of bowls, one for inside and one for outside, depending on where the dog will be fed and where he will be spending most of his time. Stainless steel or sturdy plastic bowls are popular choices. Although plastic bowls are more chewable, dogs tend not to chew on the steel variety, which can also be sterilised. Some dog owners like to put their dogs' food and water bowls on specially made elevated stands; this brings the food closer to the dog's level so he does not have to bend down as far, thus aiding his digestion and helping to guard against bloat or gastric torsion in deep-chested dogs. The most important thing is to buy sturdy bowls since, again, anything is in danger of being chewed by puppy teeth and you do not want your dog to be constantly chewing apart his bowl (for his safety and for your wallet!).

PUPPY-PROOFING YOUR HOME

Aside from making sure that your Rottweiler will be comfortable in your home, you also have to make sure that your home is safe for your

Pet shops have large varieties of leads in different lengths, strengths, colours and materials. Get a top-quality lead, as it will be useful for the entire life of the dog.

CLEANING SUPPLIES

A pup that is not housetrained means you will be doing a lot of cleaning until he is. Accidents will occur, which is okay for now

keep all household cleaners and chemicals where the pup cannot get to them.

It is just as important to make sure that the outside of your home is safe. Of course your puppy should never be unsupervised, but a pup let loose in the garden will want to run and explore, and he should be granted that freedom. Do not let a fence give you a false sense of security; you would be surprised how crafty (and persistent) a dog can be in figuring out how to dig under and squeeze his way through small holes, or to jump or climb over a fence. The remedy is to make the fence high enough so that it really is impossible for your dog to get over it (about 3 metres should suffice), and well embedded into the ground. Be sure to repair or secure any gaps in the fence. Check the fence periodically to ensure that it is in good shape and make repairs as needed; a very determined pup may return to the same spot to 'work on it' until he is able to get through.

Food and water bowls are essential for the proper care of your Rottweiler.

Rottweiler. This means taking precautions to make sure that your pup will not get into anything he should not get into and that there is nothing within his reach that may harm him should he sniff it, chew it, inspect it, etc. This probably seems obvious since, while you are primarily concerned with your pup's safety, at the same time you do not want your belongings to be ruined. Breakables should be placed out of reach if your dog is to have full run of the house. If he is to be limited to certain places within the house, keep any potentially dangerous items in the 'off-limits' areas. An electrical cord can pose a danger should the puppy decide to taste it—and who is going to convince a pup that it would not make a great chew toy? Cords should be kept from puppy's teeth and fastened tightly against the wall. If your dog is going to spend time in a crate, make sure that there is nothing near his crate that he can reach if he sticks his curious little nose or paws through the openings. And just as you would with a child,

FIRST TRIP TO THE VET
Okay, you have picked out your puppy, your home and family are ready, now all you have to do is pick your Rottweiler up from the breeder and the fun begins, right? Well...not so fast. Something else you need to prepare for is your pup's first trip to the veterinary surgeon. Perhaps the breeder can recommend someone in the area that specialises in Rottweilers, or maybe

you know some other Rottweiler owners who can suggest a good vet. Either way, you should have an appointment arranged for your pup before you pick him up; plan on taking him for a checkup within the first few days of bringing him home.

The garden or kennel run in which your Rottweiler is kept should be securely fenced in.

The pup's first visit will consist of an overall examination to make sure that the pup does not have any problems that are not apparent to the eye. The veterinary surgeon will also set up a schedule for the pup's vaccinations; the breeder will inform you of which ones the pup has already received and the vet can continue from there.

INTRODUCTION TO THE FAMILY
Everyone in the house will be excited about the puppy coming home and will want to pet him and play with him, but it is best to make the introduction low-key so as not to overwhelm the puppy. He is apprehensive already; it is the first time he has been separated from his mother and the breeder, and the

ride to your home is likely the first time he has been in a car. The last thing you want to do is smother him, as this will only frighten him further. This is not to say that human contact is not extremely necessary at this stage, because this is the time when an instant connection between the pup and his human family is formed. Gentle petting and soothing words should help console him, as well as just putting him down and letting him explore on his own (under your watchful eye, of course).

The pup may approach the family members or may busy himself with exploring for a while. Gradually, each person should spend some time with the pup, one at a time, crouching down to get as close to the pup's level as possible and letting him sniff their hands and petting him gently. He definitely needs human attention and he needs to be touched—this is

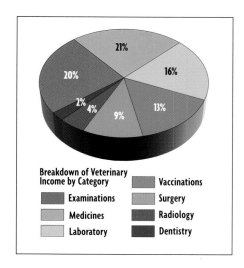

Breakdown of Veterinary Income by Category

- Examinations
- Medicines
- Laboratory
- Vaccinations
- Surgery
- Radiology
- Dentistry

how to form an immediate bond. Just remember that the pup is experiencing a lot of things for the first time, all at the same time. There are new people, new noises, new smells, and new things to investigate; so be gentle, be affectionate and be as comforting as you can be.

YOUR PUP'S FIRST NIGHT HOME
You have travelled home with your new charge safely in his basket or crate. He has been to the vet for a thorough check-over; he has been weighed, his papers examined; perhaps he has even been vaccinated and wormed as well. He has met the family, licked the whole family, including the excited children and the less-than-happy cat. He has explored his area, his new bed, the garden and anywhere else he has been permitted. He has eaten his first meal at home and relieved himself in the proper place. He has heard lots of new sounds, smelled new friends and seen more of the outside world than ever before.

That was the just the first day! He is exhausted and is ready for bed...or so you think!

It is puppy's first night and you are ready to say 'Good night'—keep in mind that this is puppy's first night ever to be sleeping alone. His dam and littermates are no longer at paw's length and he is a bit scared, cold and lonely. Be reassuring to your new family member. This is not the time to spoil him and give in to his inevitable whining.

Puppies whine. They whine to let the others know where they are and hopefully to get company out of it. Place your pup in his new bed or crate in his room and close the door. Mercifully, he will fall asleep without a peep. If the inevitable occurs, ignore the whining; he is fine. Be strong and keep his interest in mind. Do not allow your heart to become guilty and visit the pup. He will fall asleep.

A toy may help keep your puppy occupied and less prone to whining, nipping or other undesirable behaviour.

Many breeders recommend placing a piece of bedding from his former homestead in his new bed so that he recognises the scent of his littermates. Others still advise placing a hot water bottle in his bed for warmth. This latter may be a good idea provided the pup does not attempt to suckle—he will get good and wet and may not fall asleep so fast.

Puppy's first night can be somewhat stressful for the pup and his new family. Remember that you are setting the tone of nighttime at your house. Unless you want to play with your pup every evening at 10 p.m., midnight and 2 a.m., do

Provide your Rottweiler with comfortable bedding. A dog in the wild would use leaves as a burrow, but a pet dog needs a proper dog bed or a blanket in a crate.

not initiate the habit. Surely your family will thank you, and so will your pup!

PREVENTING PUPPY PROBLEMS
SOCIALISATION

Now that you have done all of the preparatory work and have helped your pup get accustomed to his new home and family, it is about time for you to have some fun! Socialising your Rottweiler pup gives you the opportunity to show off your new friend, and your pup gets to reap the benefits of being an adorable furry creature that people will adore, want

The toughest night with your Rottweiler puppy will be the first night, for both the puppy and the family.

to pet and, in general, think is absolutely precious!

Besides getting to know his new family, your puppy should be

The majority of problems that are commonly seen in young pups will disappear as your Rottweiler gets older. However, how you deal with problems when he is young will determine how he reacts to discipline as an adult dog. It is important to establish who is boss (hopefully it will be you!) right away when you are first bonding with your Rottweiler. This bond will set the tone for the rest of your life together.

exposed to other people, animals and situations. This will help him become well adjusted as he grows up and less prone to being timid or fearful of the new things he will encounter. Your pup's socialisation began at the breeder's, now it is your responsibility to continue. The socialisation he receives up until the age of 12 weeks is the most critical, as this is the time when he forms his impressions of the outside world. Lack of socialisation can manifest itself in fear and aggression as the dog grows up. He needs lots of human contact, affection, handling and exposure to other animals. Be careful during the eight-to-ten-week period, also known as the fear period. The interaction he receives during this time should be gentle and reassuring.

Once your pup has received his necessary vaccinations, feel free to take him out and about (on his lead, of course). Take him around the neighbourhood, take him on your daily errands, let people pet him, let him meet other dogs and pets, etc. Puppies do not have to try to make friends; there will be no short-age of people who will want to introduce themselves. Just make sure that you carefully supervise each meeting. If the neighbourhood children want to say hello, for example, that is great—children and pups most often make great com-panions. But sometimes an excited child can unintentionally handle a pup too roughly, or an overzealous pup can playfully nip a little too hard. You want to make socialisa-tion experiences positive ones; what a pup learns during this very forma-tive stage will impact his attitude toward future encounters. A pup

Thorough socialisation includes not only meeting new people but also being introduced to new experiences such as riding in the car, having his coat brushed, hearing the television, walking in a crowd—the list is endless. The more your pup experiences, and the more positive the experiences are, the less of a shock and the less scary it will be for your pup to encounter new things.

that has a bad experience with a child may grow up to be a dog that is shy around or aggressive toward children, and you want your dog to be comfortable around everyone.

CONSISTENCY IN TRAINING
Dogs, being pack animals, naturally need a leader, or else they try to establish dominance in their packs. When you bring a dog into your family, who becomes the leader and who becomes the 'pack' are entirely up to you! Your pup's intuitive quest for dominance, coupled with the fact that it is nearly impossible to look at an adorable Rottweiler pup, with his 'puppy-dog' eyes and his too-big-for-his-head-still-floppy ears, and not cave in, give the pup almost an unfair advantage in get-ting the upper hand! And a pup will definitely test the waters to see what he can and cannot get away with. Do not give in to those plead-ing eyes—stand your ground when it comes to disciplining the pup and make sure that all family members do the same. It will only confuse the pup when Mother tells him to get off the couch when he is used to sitting up there with Father to watch the nightly news. Avoid dis-crepancies by having all members of the household decide on the rules before the pup even comes home...and be consistent in enforc-ing them! Early training shapes the dog's personality, so you cannot be unclear in what you expect.

Playtime with the children is fun for all—just provide the neces-sary super-vision.

57

COMMON PUPPY PROBLEMS

The best way to prevent problems is to be proactive in stopping an undesirable behaviour as soon as it starts. The old saying 'You can't teach an old dog new tricks' does not necessarily hold true, but it is true that it is much easier to discourage bad behaviour in a young developing pup than to wait until the pup's bad behaviour becomes the adult dog's bad habit. There are some problems that are especially prevalent in puppies as they develop.

'You can't teach an old dog new tricks' is an untrue expression, but it is easier to train a pup.

NIPPING

As puppies start to teethe, they feel the need to sink their teeth into anything...unfortunately that includes your fingers, arms, hair, toes...whatever happens to be available. You may find this behaviour cute for about the first five seconds...until you feel just how sharp those puppy teeth are. This is something you want to discourage immediately and consistently with a firm 'No!' (or whatever number of firm 'No's' it takes for him to understand that you mean business) and replace your finger with an appropriate chew toy. While this behaviour is mere-

ly annoying when the dog is still young, it can become dangerous as your Rottweiler's adult teeth grow in and his jaws develop, if he thinks that it is okay to gnaw on human appendages. You do not want to take a chance with a Rottweiler, this is a breed whose jaws become naturally very strong. He

---

DID YOU KNOW?

Chewing goes hand in hand with nipping in the sense that a teething puppy is always looking for a way to soothe his aching gums. In this case, instead of chewing on you, he may have taken a liking to your favourite shoe or something else which he should not be chewing. Again, realise that this is a normal canine behaviour that does not need to be discouraged, only redirected. Your pup just needs to be taught what is acceptable to chew on and what is off limits. Consistently tell him NO when you catch him chewing on something forbidden and give him a chew toy. Conversely, praise him when you catch him chewing on something appropriate. In this way you are discouraging the inappropriate behaviour and reinforcing the desired behaviour. The puppy chewing should stop after his adult teeth have come in, but most adult dogs continue to chew for various reasons—perhaps because he is bored, perhaps to relieve tension, or perhaps he just likes to chew. That is why it is important to redirect his chewing when he is still young.

does not mean any harm with a friendly nip, but he also does not know his own strength.

CRYING/WHINING

Your pup will often cry, whine, whimper, howl or make some type of commotion when he is left alone. This is basically his way of calling out for attention, of calling out to make sure that you know he is there and that you have not forgotten about him. He feels insecure when he is left alone, for example, when you are out of the house and he is in his crate or when you are in another part of the house and he cannot see you. The noise he is making is an expression of the anxiety he feels at being alone, so he needs to be taught that being alone is okay. You are not actually training the dog to stop making noise, you are training him to feel comfortable when he is alone and thus removing the need for him to make the noise. This is where the crate filled with cosy blankets and a toy comes in handy. You want to know that he is safe when you are not there to supervise, and you know that he will be safe in his crate rather than roaming freely about the house. In order for the pup to stay in his crate without making a fuss, he needs to be comfortable in his crate. On that note, it is extremely important that the crate is never used as a form of punishment, or the pup

A puppy looks to and trusts his owner for care and guidance.

will have a negative association with the crate.

Accustom the pup to the crate in short, gradually increasing time intervals in which you put him in the crate, maybe with a treat, and stay in the room with him. If he cries or makes a fuss, do not go to him, but stay in his sight. Gradually he will realise that staying in his crate is all right without your help, and it will not be so traumatic for him when you are not around. You may want to leave the radio on softly when you leave the house; the sound of human voices may be comforting to him.

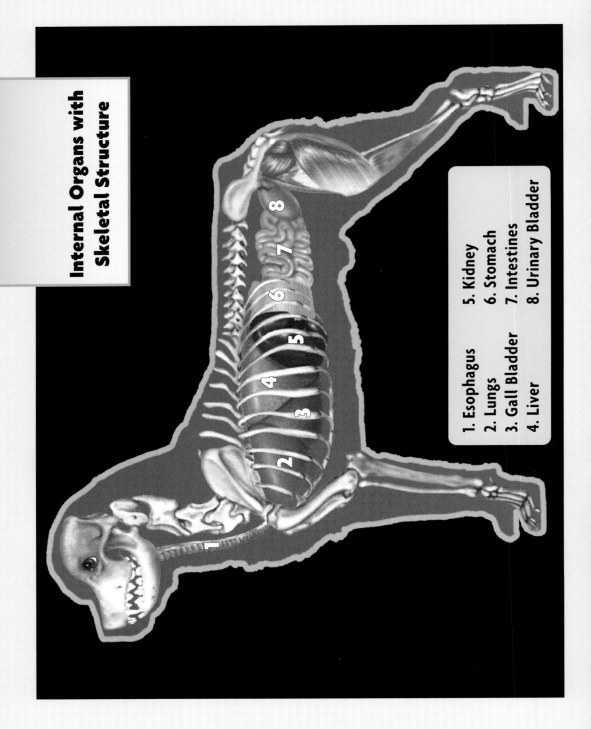

Internal Organs with Skeletal Structure

1. Esophagus   5. Kidney
2. Lungs   6. Stomach
3. Gall Bladder   7. Intestines
4. Liver   8. Urinary Bladder

Everyday Care of Your Rottweiler

DIETARY AND FEEDING CONSIDERATIONS

In today's world, your Rottweiler has hundreds of choices for eating. The market offers dozens of brands in dozens of varieties: from the puppy diet lamb and rice to the senior diet to the hypoallergenic to the low-calorie! Since your Rottweiler's nutrition is related to his coat and health and temperament, you want to offer him the best possible diet, fit for a Rottweiler his age. Dedicated owners, however, can become very perplexed by the vast number of choices. Even those people who truly want to feed their dogs the best often cannot do so because they do not know which foods are best for their dog.

Dog foods are produced in three basic types: dried, semi-moist and canned or tinned. Dried foods are for the cost conscious because they are much less expensive than semi-moist and canned. Dried foods contain the least fat and the most preservatives. Most tinned foods are 60–70-percent water, while semi-moist foods are so full of sugar that they are the least preferred by owners, though dogs welcome them (as does a child sweets).

Three stages of development must be considered when selecting a diet for your dog: the puppy stage, the mid-age or adult stage and the senior age or geriatric stage.

PUPPY STAGE

Puppies have a natural instinct to suck milk from their mother's breasts. They should exhibit this

behaviour the first day of their lives. If they don't suckle within a few hours you should attempt to put them onto their mother's nipple. Their failure to feed means you have to feed them yourself under the advice and guidance of a veterinary surgeon. This will involve a baby bottle and a special formula. Their mother's milk is much better than any formula because it contains colostrum, a sort of antibiotic milk which protects the puppy during the first eight to ten weeks of their lives.

Follow the advice of your vet or the breeder from whom you bought your Rottweiler when it comes to food.

61

Puppies should be allowed to nurse for six weeks and they should be slowly weaned away from their mother by introducing small portions of tinned meat after they are about one month old.

A Rottweiler isn't considered an adult until he stops growing.

By the time they are eight weeks old, they should be completely weaned and fed solely a puppy dried food. During this weaning period, their diet is most important as the puppy grows fastest during its first year of life. Growth foods can be recommended by your veterinary surgeon and the puppy should be kept on this diet for up to 18 months.

Puppy diets should be balanced for your dog's needs and supplements of vitamins, minerals and protein should not be necessary.

ADULT DIETS

A dog is considered an adult when it has stopped growing. The growth is in height and/or length. Do not consider the dog's weight when the decision is made to switch from a puppy diet to a maintenance diet. Again you should rely upon your veterinary

A shiny coat and alert demeanour are two signs that your Rott-weiler is getting the proper nutrition.

surgeon to recommend an acceptable maintenance diet. Major dog food manufacturers specialise in this type of food and it is just necessary for you to select the one best suited to your dog's needs. Active dogs may have different requirements than sedate dogs.

A Rottweiler reaches adulthood at about two years of age, though some dogs fully mature at 16 months, while others may take up to three years.

DIETS FOR SENIOR DOGS

As dogs get older, their metabolism changes. The older dog usually exercises less, moves more slowly and sleeps more. This change in lifestyle and physiological performance requires a change in diet. Since these changes take place slowly, they might not be recognisable.

WATER

Just as your dog needs proper nutrition from his food, water is an essential 'nutrient' as well. Water keeps the dog's body properly hydrated and promotes normal function of the body's systems. During housebreaking it is necessary to keep an eye on how much water your Rottweiler is drinking, but once he is reliably trained he should have access to clean fresh water at all times. Make sure that the dog's water bowl is clean, and change the water often. As some vets have recommended, do not leave water bowls down when feeding your dog. This practice can help to promote the onset of bloat in the Rottweiler.

EXERCISE

Exercising a Rottweiler is not as daunting as it may seem. The Rottweiler is a working dog, not a

Watching a litter of Rottweilers eat from the same bowl will tell you a lot about the pups' individual personalities.

What is easily recognisable is weight gain. By continually feeding your dog an adult maintenance diet when it is slowing down metabolically, your dog will gain weight. Obesity in an older dog compounds the health problems that already accompany old age.

As your dog gets older, few of their organs function up to par. The kidneys slow down and the intestines become less efficient. These age-related factors are best handled with a change in diet and a change in feeding schedule to give smaller portions that are more easily digested.

There is no single best diet for every older dog. While many dogs do well on light or senior diets, other dogs do better on puppy diets or other special premium diets such as lamb and rice.

Be sensitive to your senior Rottweiler's diet and this will help control other problems that may arise with your old friend.

Many adult diets are based on grain. There is nothing wrong with this as long as it does not contain soy meal. Diets based on soy will often cause flatulence (passing wind).

Grain-based diets are almost always the least expensive and a good grain diet is just as good as the most expensive diet containing animal protein.

There are many cases, however, when your dog might require a special diet. These special requirements should only be recommended by your veterinary surgeon.

What are you feeding your dog?

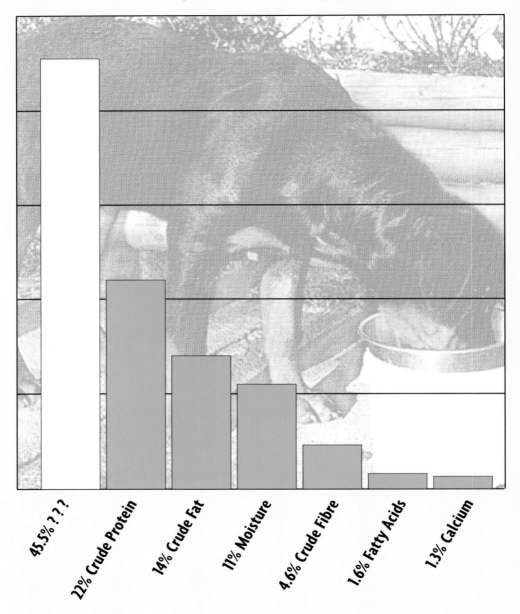

45.5% ? ? ? ?.

22% Crude Protein

14% Crude Fat

11% Moisture

4.6% Crude Fibre

1.6% Fatty Acids

1.3% Calcium

Read the label on your dog food. Most manufacturers merely advise you of 50-55% of the contents, leaving the other 45% in doubt.

field dog that has pent-up energy or a track dog that has long legs to stretch. All dogs require some form of exercise, regardless of breed. A sedentary lifestyle is as harmful to a dog as it is to a person. The Rottweiler happens to be a fairly active breed that requires more exercise than, say, an English Bulldog, but you don't have to be a weightlifter or marathon runner to provide your dog with the exercise he needs. Regular walks, play sessions in the garden, and letting the dog run free in the garden under your supervision are all sufficient forms of exercise for the Rottweiler. For those who are more ambitious, you will find that your Rottweiler will be able to keep up with you on extra long walks or the morning run. Not only is exercise essential to keep the dog's body fit, it is essential to his mental well-being. A bored dog will find something to do, which often manifests itself in some type of destructive behaviour. In this sense, it is essential for the owner's mental well-being as well!

GROOMING
BRUSHING
A natural bristle brush, a slicker brush, or even a hound glove can be used for regular routine brushing. Grooming is effective for removing dead hair and stimulating the dog's natural oils to add shine and a healthy look to the coat. Your Rottweiler is not a

breed that needs excessive grooming, but his coat needs to be brushed every few days as part of routine maintenance. Regular brushing will get rid of dust and dandruff and remove any dead hair. Regular grooming sessions are also a good way to spend time with your dog. Many dogs grow to like the feel of being brushed and will enjoy the daily routine.

BATHING
Dogs do not need to be bathed as often as humans, but occasional bathing is essential for healthy skin and a healthy, shiny coat.

A once-over with a glove like this one will give your Rottweiler's black coat polish and shine.

Again, like most anything, if you accustom your pup to being bathed as a puppy, it will be second nature by the time he grows up. You want your dog to be at

Cutting the Rottweiler's nails should be a routine task for the owner, though any dog groomer will happily perform the task for you.

ease in the bath or else it could end up a wet, soapy, messy ordeal for both of you!

Brush your Rottweiler thoroughly before wetting his coat. This will get rid of most of the dead coat. Make sure that your dog has a good non-slip surface to stand on. Begin by wetting the dog's coat. A shower or hose attachment is necessary for thoroughly wetting and rinsing the coat. Check the water temperature to make sure that it is neither too hot nor too cold.

Grooming your Rottweiler should be a pleasure and not a chore.

Next, apply shampoo to the dog's coat and work it into a good lather. You should purchase a shampoo that is made for dogs; do

The use of human soap products like shampoo, bubble bath and hand soap can be damaging to a dog's coat and skin. Human products are too strong and remove the protective oils coating the dog's hair and skin (making him water-resistant). Use only shampoo made especially for dogs and you may like to use a medicated shampoo which will always help to keep external parasites at bay.

not use a product made for human hair. Wash the head last; you do not want shampoo to drip into the dog's eyes while you are washing the rest of his body. Work the shampoo all the way down to the skin. You can use this opportunity to check the skin for any bumps, bites or other abnormalities. Do not neglect any area of the body—get all of the hard-to-reach places.

Once the dog has been thoroughly shampooed, he requires an equally thorough rinsing. Shampoo left in the coat can be irritating to the skin. Protect his eyes from the shampoo by shielding them with your hand and directing the flow of water in the opposite direction. You should also avoid getting water in the ear canal. Be prepared for your dog to shake out his coat—you might want to stand back, but make sure you have a hold on the dog to keep him from running through the house.

EAR CLEANING

The ears should be kept clean and any excess hair inside the ear should be trimmed. Ears can be cleaned with a cotton wipes and special cleaner or ear powder made especially for dogs. Be on the lookout for any signs of infection or ear mite infestation. If your Rottweiler has been shaking his head or scratching at his ears frequently, this usually indicates a problem. If his ears have an unusual odour, this is a sure sign of mite infestation or infection, and a signal to have his ears checked by the veterinary surgeon.

NAIL CLIPPING

Your Rottweiler should be accustomed to having his nails trimmed at an early age, since it will be part of your maintenance routine throughout his life. Not only does it look nicer, but a dog with long nails can cause injury if he jumps up or if he scratches someone unintentionally. Also, a long nail has a better chance of ripping and bleeding, or causing the feet to

Once you are sure that the dog is thoroughly rinsed, squeeze the excess water out of the coat with your hand and dry him with a heavy towel. You may choose to blow-dry his coat or just let it dry naturally. In cold weather, never allow your dog outside with a wet coat.

There are 'dry bath' products on the market, which are sprays and powders intended for spot cleaning, that can be used between regular baths, if necessary. They are not substitutes for regular baths, but they are easy to use for touch-ups as they do not require rinsing.

spread. A good rule of thumb is that if you can hear your dog's nails clicking on the floor when he walks, his nails are too long.

Before you start cutting, make sure you can identify the 'quick' in each nail. The quick is a blood vessel that runs through the centre of each nail and grows rather close to the end. It will bleed if accidentally cut, which will be quite painful for the dog as it contains nerve endings. Keep some type of clotting agent on hand, such as a styptic pencil or styptic powder (the type used for shaving). This will stop the bleeding quickly when applied to the end of the cut nail. Do not panic if this happens, just stop the bleeding and talk soothingly to your dog. Once he has calmed down, move

Rottweilers frequently love the water and will voluntarily welcome the opportunity to cool off on a hot day.

67

A dog that spends a lot of time outside on a hard surface such as cement or pavement will have his nails naturally worn down and may not need to have them trimmed as often, except maybe in the colder months when he is not outside as much. Regardless, it is best to get your Rottweiler accustomed to this procedure at an early age so that he is used to it. Some dogs are especially sensitive about having their feet touched, but if a dog has experienced it since he was young, he should not be bothered by it.

Your Rottweiler should become accustomed to car travel and the crate that is associated with it.

on to the next nail. It is better to clip a little at a time, particularly with black-nailed dogs.

Hold your pup steady as you begin trimming his nails; you do not want him to make any sudden movements or run away. Talk to him soothingly and stroke his fur as you clip. Holding his foot in your hand, simply take off the end of each nail in one quick clip. You can purchase nail clippers that are specially made for dogs; you can probably find them wherever you buy pet or grooming supplies.

TRAVELLING WITH YOUR DOG
CAR TRAVEL
You should accustom your Rottweiler to riding in an car at an early age. You may or may not often take him in the car, but at the very least he will need to go to the vet and you do not want these

trips to be traumatic for the dog or a big hassle for you. The safest way for a dog to ride in the car is in his crate. If he uses a fibreglass crate in the house, you can use the same crate for travel. If you have a wire crate in the house, consider purchasing an appropriately sized fibreglass or wooden crate for travelling. Wire crates can be used for travel, but fibreglass or wooden crates are safer.

Put the pup in the crate and see how he reacts. If he seems uneasy, you can have a passenger hold him on his lap while you drive. Another option is a specially made safety harness for dogs, which straps the dog in much like a seat belt. Do not let the dog roam loose in the vehicle—this is *very* dangerous! If you should stop short, your dog can be thrown and injured. If the dog starts climbing on you and pester-

ing you while you are driving, you will not be able to concentrate on the road. It is an unsafe situation for everyone—human and canine.

For long trips, be prepared to stop to let the dog relieve himself. Bring along whatever you need to clean up after him. You should bring along some old towels and rags, should he have an accident in the car or become carsick.

AIR TRAVEL

Whilst it is possible to take a dog on a flight within Britain, this is fairly unusual and advance permission is always required. The dog will be required to travel in a fibreglass crate and you should always check in advance with the airline regarding specific requirements. To help the dog be at ease, put one of his favourite toys in the crate with him. Do not feed the dog for at least six hours before the trip to minimise his need to relieve himself. However, certain regulations specify that water must always be made available to the dog in the crate.

Make sure your dog is properly identified and that your contact information appears on his ID tags and on his crate. Animals travel in a different area of the plane than human passengers, and, although transporting animals is routine for many air-

lines, there is always that slight risk of getting separated from your dog.

Your Rottweiler should wear his collar with ID tags all the time.

BOARDING

So you want to take a family holiday—and you want to include all members of the family. You would probably make arrangements for accommodations ahead of time anyway, but this is especially important when travelling with a dog. You do not want to make an overnight stop at the

If your dog gets lost, he is not able to ask for directions home.

Identification tags fastened to the collar give important information—the dog's name, the owner's name, the owner's address and a telephone number where the owner can be reached. This makes it easy for whoever finds the dog to contact the owner and arrange to have the dog returned. An added advantage is that a person will be more likely to approach a lost dog who has ID tags on his collar; it tells the person that this is somebody's pet rather than a stray. This is the easiest and fastest method of identification provided that the tags stay on the collar and the collar stays on the dog.

For international travel you will have to make arrangements well in advance (perhaps months), as countries' regulations pertaining to bringing in animals differ. There may be special health certificates and/or vaccinations that your dog will need before taking the trip, sometimes this has to be done within a certain time frame. In rabies-free countries, you will need to bring proof of the dog's rabies vaccination and there may be a quarantine period upon arrival.

only place around for miles to find out that they do not allow dogs. Also, you do not want to reserve a place for your family without mentioning that you are bringing a dog, because if it is against their policy you may not have a place to stay.

Alternatively, if you are travelling and choose not to bring your Rottweiler, you will have to make arrangements for him while you are away. Some options are to bring him to a neighbour's house to stay while you are gone, to have a trusted neighbour stop

Never leave your dog alone in the car. In hot weather your dog can die from the high temperature inside a closed vehicle; even a car parked in the shade can heat up very quickly. Leaving the window open is dangerous as well since the dog can hurt himself trying to get out.

by often or stay at your house, or bring your dog to a reputable boarding kennel. If you choose to board him at a kennel, you should stop by to see the facility and where the dogs are kept to make sure that it is clean. Talk to some of the employees and see how they treat the dogs—do they spend time with the dogs, play with them, exercise them, etc.? You know that your Rottweiler will not be happy unless he gets regular activity. Also find out the kennel's policy on vaccinations and what they require. This is for all of the dogs' safety, since when dogs are kept together, there is a greater risk of diseases being passed from dog to dog. Most facilities require owners to provide current proof of vaccination.

IDENTIFICATION
Your Rottweiler is your valued companion and friend. That is why you always keep a close eye on him and you have made sure that he cannot escape from the garden or wriggle out of his collar and run away from you. However, accidents can happen and there may come a time when your dog unexpectedly gets separated from you. If this unfortunate event should occur, the first thing on your mind will be finding him. Proper identification will increase the chances of his being returned to you safely and quickly.

Housebreaking and Training Your Rottweiler

Living with an untrained dog is a lot like owning a piano that you do not know how to play—it is a nice object to look at but it does not do much more than that to bring you pleasure. Now try taking piano lessons and suddenly the piano comes alive and brings forth magical sounds and rhythms that set your heart singing and your body swaying.

The same is true with your Rottweiler. At first you enjoy seeing him around the house. He does not do much with you other than to need food, water and exercise. Come to think of it, he does not bring you much joy, either. He is a big responsibility with a very small return. And often, he develops unacceptable behaviours that annoy and/or infuriate you to say nothing of bad habits that may end up costing you great sums of money. Not a good thing!

Now train your Rottweiler. Enrol in an obedience class. Teach him good manners as you learn how and why he behaves the way he does. Find out how to communicate with your dog and how to recognise and understand his communications with you. Suddenly the dog takes on a new role in your life—he is smart, interesting, well behaved and fun to be with, and he demonstrates his bond of devotion to you daily. In other words, your Rottweiler does wonders for your ego because he constantly reminds you that you are not only his leader, you are his hero! Miraculous things have happened— you have a wonderful dog (even your family and friends have noticed the transformation!) and you feel good about yourself.

Those involved with teaching dog obedience and counselling owners about their dogs' behaviour have discovered some interesting facts about dog ownership. For example, training dogs when they are puppies results in the highest rate of success in developing well-mannered and

Obedience training your Rottweiler is an absolute necessity. This dog knows the house rules and waits patiently for someone to let him back in.

well-adjusted adult dogs. Training an older dog, say from six months to six years of age, can produce almost equal results providing that the owner accepts the dog's slower rate of learning capability and is willing to work patiently to help the dog

Puppies are naturally curious and exuberant.

succeed at developing to his fullest potential. Unfortunately, the patience factor is what many owners of untrained adult dogs lack, so they do not persist until their dogs are successful at learning particular behaviours.

Puppy teeth are fine and sharp, which is one of the reasons that nipping should be discouraged early on.

Training a puppy, for example, aged 8 to 16 weeks (20 weeks at the most) is like working with a dry sponge in a pool of water. The pup soaks up whatever you show him and constantly looks for more things to do and learn. At this early age, his body is not yet producing hormones, and therein lies the reason for such a high rate of success. Without hormones, he is focused on his owners and not particularly interested in investigating other places, dogs, people, etc. You are his leader; his provider of food, water, shelter and security. Therefore, he latches onto you and wants to stay close. He will usually follow you from room to room, will not let you out of his

sight when you are outdoors with him, and respond in like manner to the people and animals you encounter. If, for example, you greet a friend warmly, he will be happy to greet the person as well. If, however, you are hesitant, even anxious, about the approach of a stranger, he will respond accordingly.

Once the puppy begins to produce hormones, his natural curiosity emerges and he begins to investigate the world around him. It is at that time when you may notice that the untrained dog begins to wander away from you and even ignore your commands to stay close. When this behaviour becomes a problem, the owner has two choices: get rid of the dog or train him. It is strongly urged that you choose the latter option.

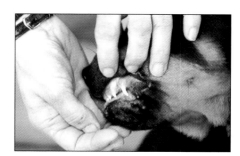

Occasionally there are no classes available within a reasonable distance from the owner's home. Sometimes there are classes available but the tuition is too costly. Whatever the circumstances, the solution to the problem of lack of lesson availability lies within the pages of this book.

This chapter is devoted to helping you train your Rottweiler at home. If the recommended procedures are followed faithfully, you may expect positive results that will prove rewarding to both you and your dog.

Whether your Rottweiler is a puppy or a mature adult, the methods of teaching and the techniques we use in training basic behaviours are the same. After all, no dog, whether puppy or adult,

likes harsh or inhumane methods. All creatures, however, respond favourably to gentle motivational methods and sincere praise and encouragement. Now let us get started.

HOUSEBREAKING

You can train a puppy to relieve itself wherever you choose. For example, city dwellers often train their puppies to relieve themselves in the gutter because large plots of grass are not readily available. Suburbanites, on the other hand, usually have gardens to accommodate their dogs' needs.

If you have other pets in the home and/or interact often with the pets of friends and other family members, your pup will respond to those pets in much the same manner as you do. It is only when you show fear or resentment toward another animal that he will act fearful or unfriendly.

Outdoor training includes such surfaces as grass, dirt and cement. Indoor training usually means training your dog to newspaper.

When deciding on the surface and location that you will want your Rottweiler to use, be sure it is going to be permanent. Training your dog to grass and then changing your mind two months later is extremely difficult for both dog and owner.

Next, choose the command you will use each and every time you want your puppy to void. 'Go hurry up' and 'Toilet' are examples of commands commonly used by dog owners.

Get in the habit of asking the puppy, 'Do you want to go hurry up?' (or whatever your chosen relief command is) before you take him out. That way, when he becomes an adult, you will be able to determine

The great outdoors means unexplored territory for a pup— keep a close eye on him as he familiarises himself with the garden.

Your dog is actually training you at the same time you are training him. Dogs do things to get attention. They usually repeat whatever succeeds in getting your attention. Be sure to reward good behaviour with lavish praise and attention.

if he wants to go out when you ask him. A confirmation will be signs of interest, wagging his tail, watching you intently, going to the door, etc.

PUPPY'S NEEDS

A Rottweiler cooling off in a bathtub during a dog show on a hot day. Several show societies provide bath tubs for this purpose during the summer months.

Puppy needs to relieve himself after play periods, after each meal, after he has been sleeping and any time he indicates that he is looking for a place to urinate or defecate.

The urinary and intestinal tract muscles of very young puppies are not fully developed. Therefore, like human babies, puppies need to relieve themselves frequently.

Take your puppy out often—every hour for an eight-week-old, for example. The older the puppy, the less often he will need to relieve himself. Finally, as a mature healthy adult, he will require only three to five relief trips per day.

HOUSING

Since the types of housing and control you provide for your puppy has a direct relationship on the success

A basic obedience beginner's class usually lasts for six to eight weeks. Dog and owner attend an hour-long lesson once a week and practise for a few minutes, several times a day, each day at home. If done properly, the whole procedure will result in a well-mannered dog and an owner who delights in living with a pet that is eager to please and enjoys doing things with his owner.

of housetraining, we consider the various aspects of both before we begin training.

Bringing a new puppy home and turning him loose in your house can

be compared to turning a child loose in a sports arena and telling the child that the place is all his! The sheer enormity of the place would be too much for him to handle.

Instead, offer the puppy clearly defined areas where he can play, sleep, eat and live. A room of the house where the family gathers is the most obvious choice. Puppies are social animals and need to feel a part of the pack right from the start. Hearing your voice, watching you while you are doing things and smelling you nearby are all positive reinforcers that he is now a member of your pack. Usually a family room, the kitchen or a nearby adjoining

Canine Development Schedule

It is important to understand how and at what age a puppy develops into adulthood. If you are a puppy owner, consult the following Canine Development Schedule to determine the stage of development your Rottweiler puppy is currently experiencing. This knowledge will help you as you work with the puppy in the weeks and months ahead.

Period	Age	Characteristics
FIRST TO THIRD	**BIRTH TO SEVEN WEEKS**	Puppy needs food, sleep and warmth, and responds to simple and gentle touching. Needs mother for security and disciplining. Needs litter mates for learning and interacting with other dogs. Pup learns to function within a pack and learns pack order of dominance. Begin socialising with adults and children for short periods. Begins to become aware of its environment.
FOURTH	**EIGHT TO TWELVE WEEKS**	Brain is fully developed. Needs socialising with outside world. Remove from mother and littermates. Needs to change from canine pack to human pack. Human dominance necessary. Fear period occurs between 8 and 16 weeks. Avoid fright and pain.
FIFTH	**THIRTEEN TO SIXTEEN WEEKS**	Training and formal obedience should begin. Less association with other dogs, more with people, places, situations. Period will pass easily if you remember this is pup's change-to-adolescence time. Be firm and fair. Flight instinct prominent. Permissiveness and over-disciplining can do permanent damage. Praise for good behaviour.
JUVENILE	**FOUR TO EIGHT MONTHS**	Another fear period about 7 to 8 months of age. It passes quickly, but be cautious of fright and pain. Sexual maturity reached. Dominant traits established. Dog should understand sit, down, come and stay by now.

NOTE: THESE ARE APPROXIMATE TIME FRAMES. ALLOW FOR INDIVIDUAL DIFFERENCES IN PUPPIES.

breakfast nook is ideal for providing safety and security for both puppy and owner.

> Most of all, be consistent. Always take your dog to the same location, always use the same command, and always have him on lead when he is in his relief area, unless a fenced-in garden is available.
>
> By following the Success Method, your Rottweiler puppy will be completely housetrained by the time his muscle and brain development reach maturity. Keep in mind that small breeds usually mature faster than large breeds, even though large breeds like the Rottweiler grow rapidly, but all puppies should be trained by six months of age.

A thirsty dog will find a way to quench his thirst; however, a preferable alternative to the fish pond is a clean water bowl with fresh water.

Within that room there should be a smaller area which the puppy can call his own. A cubbyhole, a wire or fibreglass dog crate or a fenced (not boarded!) corner from which he can view the activities of his new family will be fine. The size of the area or crate is the key factor here. The area must be large enough for the puppy to lay down and stretch out as well as stand up without rubbing his head on the top, yet small enough so that he cannot relieve himself at one end and sleep at the other without coming into contact with his droppings.

Dogs are, by nature, clean animals and will not remain close to their relief areas unless forced to

do so. In those cases, they then become dirty dogs and usually remain that way for life.

The crate or cubby should be lined with a clean towel and offer one toy, no more. Do not put food or water in the crate, as eating and drinking will activate his digestive processes and ultimately defeat your purpose as well as make the puppy very uncomfortable as he attempts to 'hold it.'

CONTROL

By control, we mean helping the puppy to create a lifestyle pattern that will be compatible to that of his human pack (YOU!). Just as we guide little children to learn our way of life, we must show the puppy when it is time to play, eat, sleep, exercise and even entertain himself.

Your puppy should always sleep in his crate. He should also learn that, during times of household confusion and excessive human activity such as at breakfast when family members are preparing for the day, he can play by himself in relative safety and comfort in his crate. Each time you leave the puppy alone, he should be crated. Puppies are chewers. They cannot tell the difference between lamp cords, television wires, shoes, table legs, etc. Chewing into a television wire, for example, can be fatal to the puppy while a shorted wire can start a fire in the house.

If the puppy chews on the arm of the chair when he is alone, you will probably discipline him angrily when you get home. Thus, he makes the association that your coming home means he is going to be hit or punished. (He will not remember chewing up the chair and is incapable of making the association of the discipline with his naughty deed.)

Other times of excitement, such as family parties, etc., can be fun for the puppy providing he can view the activities from the security of his crate. He is not underfoot and he is not being fed all sorts of titbits that will probably cause him stomach distress, yet he still feels a part of the fun.

SCHEDULE
As stated earlier, a puppy should be taken to his relief area each time he is released from his crate, after meals, after a play session, when he first awakens in the morning (at age 8 weeks, this can mean 5 a.m.!) and whenever he indicates by circling or sniffing busily that he needs to uri-

nate or defecate. For a puppy less than ten weeks of age, a routine of taking him out every hour is neces-

Dogs don't sweat. Their tongues are used to cool their blood.

sary. As the puppy grows, he will be able to wait for longer periods of time.

Keep trips to his relief area short. Stay no more than five or six minutes and then return to the house. If he goes during that time, praise him lavishly and take him indoors immediately. If he does not, but he has an accident when you go back indoors, pick him up immediately, say 'No! No!' and return to his relief area. Wait a few minutes, then return to the house again. NEVER hit a puppy or rub his face in urine or excrement when he has an accident!

By providing sleeping and resting quarters that fit the dog, and offering frequent opportunities to relieve himself outside his quarters, the puppy quickly learns that the outdoors (or the newspaper if you are training him to paper) is the place to go when he needs to urinate or defecate. It also reinforces his innate desire to keep his sleeping quarters clean. This, in turn, helps develop the muscle control that will eventually produce a dog with clean living habits.

Success that comes by luck is usually happenstance and frequently short lived. Success that comes by well-thought-out proven methods is often more easily achieved and permanent. This is the Success Method. It is designed to give you, the puppy owner, a simple yet proven way to help your Rottweiler puppy develop clean living habits and a feeling of security in his new environment.

Once indoors, put the puppy in his crate until you have had time to clean up his accident. Then release him to the family area and watch him more closely than before. Chances are, his accident was a result of your not picking up his signal or waiting too

Water, which should be readily available, is an absolute MUST for the Rottweiler.

long before offering him the opportunity to relieve himself. NEVER hold a grudge against the puppy for accidents.

Let the puppy learn that going outdoors means it is time to relieve himself, not play. Once trained, he will be able to play indoors and out and still differentiate between the times for play versus the times for relief.

Help him develop regular hours for naps, being alone, playing by himself and just resting, all in his crate. Encourage him to entertain himself while you are busy with your activities. Let him learn that having you near is comforting, but it is not your main purpose in life to provide him with undivided attention.

Each time you put a puppy in his crate tell him, 'Crate time!' (or whatever command you choose). Soon, he will run to his crate when he hears you say those words.

In the beginning of his training, do not leave him in his crate for prolonged periods of time except during the night when everyone is sleeping. Make his experience with his crate a pleasant one and, as an adult, he will love his crate and willingly stay in it for several hours. There are millions of people who go to work every day and leave their adult dogs crated while they are away. The dogs accept this as their lifestyle and look forward to 'crate time.'

Crate training provides safety for you, the puppy and the home. It also provides the puppy with a feeling of security, and that helps the puppy achieve self-confidence and clean habits.

Remember that one of the primary ingredients in housetraining your puppy is control. Regardless of your lifestyle, there will always be occasions when you will need to have a place where your dog can stay and be happy and safe. Crate training is the answer for now and in the future.

In conclusion, a few key elements are really all you need for a successful house and crate training method—consistency, frequency, praise, control and supervision. By following these procedures with a normal, healthy puppy, you and the puppy will soon be past the stage of 'accidents' and ready to move on to a full and rewarding life together.

ROLES OF DISCIPLINE, REWARD AND PUNISHMENT
Discipline, training one to act in accordance with rules, brings order

The puppy should also have regular play and exercise sessions when he is with you or a family member. Exercise for a very young puppy can consist of a short walk around the house or garden. Playing can include fetching games with a large ball or a special raggy. (All puppies teethe and need soft things upon which to chew.) Remember to restrict play periods to indoors within his living area (the family room for example) until he is completely house-trained.

THE SUCCESS METHOD
6 Steps to Successful Crate Training

1 Tell the puppy 'Crate time!' and place him in the crate with a small treat (a piece of cheese or half of a biscuit). Let him stay in the crate for five minutes while you are in the same room. Then release him and praise lavishly. Never release him when he is fussing. Wait until he is quiet before you let him out.

2 Repeat Step 1 several times a day.

3 The next day, place the puppy in the crate as before. Let him stay there for ten minutes. Do this several times.

4 Continue building time in five-minute increments until the puppy

stays in his crate for 30 minutes with you in the room. Always take him to his relief area after prolonged periods in his crate.

5 Now go back to Step 1 and let the puppy stay in his crate for five minutes, this time while you are out of the room.

6 Once again, build crate time in five-minute increments with you out of the room. When the puppy will stay willingly in his crate (he may even fall asleep!) for 30 minutes with you out of the room, he will be ready to stay in it for several hours at a time.

Your local pet shop will have an assortment of collars. Get the one that best suits your needs. A chain collar should only be used by someone who has been instructed in its proper use.

to life. It is as simple as that. Without discipline, particularly in a group society, chaos reigns supreme and the group will eventually perish. Humans and canines are social animals and need some form of discipline in order to function effectively. They must procure food, protect their home base and their young and reproduce to keep the species going.

If there were no discipline in the lives of social animals, they would eventually die from starvation and/or predation by other stronger animals.

Never line your pup's sleeping area with newspaper. Puppy litters are usually raised on newspaper and, once in your home, the puppy will immediately associate newspaper with voiding. Never put newspaper on any floor while housetraining, as this will only confuse the puppy. If you are paper-training him, use paper in his designated relief area ONLY. Finally, restrict water intake after evening meals. Offer a few licks at a time—never let a young puppy gulp water after meals.

In the case of domestic canines, dogs need discipline in their lives in order to understand how their pack (you and other family members) function and how they must act in order to survive.

A large humane society in a highly populated area recently surveyed dog owners regarding their satisfaction with their relationships with their dogs. People who had trained their dogs were 75% more satisfied with their pets than those who had never trained their dogs.

Dr. Edward Thorndike, a psychologist, established *Thorndike's Theory of Learning*, which states that a behaviour that results in a pleasant event tends to be repeated. A behaviour that results in an unpleasant event tends not to be repeated. It is this theory on which training methods are based today. For example, if you manipulate a dog to perform a specific behaviour and reward him for doing it, he is likely to do it again because he enjoyed the end result.

Occasionally, punishment, a penalty inflicted for an offence, is necessary. The best type of punishment often comes from an outside source. For example, a child is told not to touch the stove because he may get burned. He disobeys and touches the stove. In doing so, he receives a burn. From that time on, he respects the heat of the stove and avoids contact with it. Therefore, a behaviour that results in an unpleasant event tends not to be repeated.

A good example of a dog learning the hard way is the dog who chases the house cat. He is told many times to leave the cat alone, yet he persists in teasing the cat. Then, one day he begins chasing the cat but the cat turns and swipes a claw across the dog's face, leaving him with a painful gash on his nose. The final result is that the dog stops chasing the cat.

TRAINING EQUIPMENT
COLLAR
A simple buckle collar is fine for most dogs. One who pulls mightily on the leash may require a chain choker collar. Only in the most severe cases of a dog being totally out of control is it recommended to use a prong or pinch collar, only if these and in this case only if the owner has been instructed in the proper use of such equipment. In some areas, such as the United Kingdom, these types of collars are not allowed.

LEAD
A 1- to 2-metre lead is recommended, preferably made of leather, nylon or heavy cloth. A chain lead is not recommended, as many dog owners find that the chain cuts into their hands and that switching the lead back and forth frequently between their hands is painful.

If you begin teaching the heel by taking long walks and letting the dog pull you along, he misinterprets this action as an acceptable form of taking a walk. When you pull back on the lead to counteract his pulling, he reads that tug as a signal to pull even harder!

TREATS
Have a bag of treats on hand. Something nutritious and easy to swallow works best; use a soft treat, a chunk of cheese or a piece of cooked chicken rather than a dry biscuit. By the time the dog gets done chewing a dry treat, he will forget why he is being rewarded in the first place! Using food rewards will not teach a dog to beg at the table—the only way to teach a dog to beg at the table is to give him food from the table. In training, rewarding the dog with a food treat away from the table will help him associate praise and the treats with learning new behaviours that obviously please his owner.

If your Rottweiler knows you have a treat in your hand, he won't take his eyes off you.

81

Practice Makes Perfect!
• Have training lessons with your dog every day in several short segments—three to five times a day for a few minutes at a time is ideal.
• Do not have long practice sessions. The dog will become easily bored.
• Never practise when you are tired, ill, worried or in an otherwise negative mood. This will transmit to the dog and may have an adverse effect on its performance.
  Think fun, short and above all POSITIVE! End each session on a high note, rather than a failed exercise, and make sure to give a lot of praise. Enjoy the training and help your dog enjoy it, too.

You should be able to walk, trot or run with your Rottweiler without there being any tension on the lead.

TRAINING BEGINS: ASK THE DOG A QUESTION

In order to teach your dog anything, you must first get his attention. After all, he cannot learn anything if he is looking away from you with his mind on something else.

To get his attention, ask him, 'School?' and immediately walk over to him and give him a treat as you tell him 'Good dog.' Wait a minute or two and repeat the routine, this time with a treat in your hand as you approach the dog to within a foot of him. Do not go directly to him, but stop about a foot short of him and hold out the treat as you ask, 'School?' He will see you approaching with a treat in your hand and most likely begin walking toward you. As you meet, give him the treat and praise again.

The third time, ask the question, have a treat in your hand and walk only a short distance toward the dog so that he must walk almost all the way to you. As he reaches you, give him the treat and praise again.

By this time, the dog will probably be getting the idea that if he pays attention to you, especially when you ask that question, it will pay off in treats and fun activities for him. In other words, he learns that 'school' means doing fun things with you that result in treats and positive attention for him.

Remember that the dog does not understand your verbal language, he only recognises sounds. Your question translates to a series of sounds for him, and those sounds become the signal to go to you and pay attention; if he does, he will get to interact with you plus receive treats and praise.

THE BASIC COMMANDS
TEACHING SIT
Now that you have the dog's attention, hold the lead in your left hand and the food treat in your right. Place your food hand at the dog's nose and let him lick the treat but not take it from you. Say 'Sit' and slowly raise your food hand from in front of the dog's nose up over his head so that he is looking at the ceiling. As he bends his head upward, he will have to bend his knees to maintain his balance. As he bends his knees, he will assume a sit posi-

tion. At that point, release the food treat and praise lavishly with comments such as 'Good dog! Good sit!', etc. Remember to always praise enthusiastically, because dogs relish verbal praise from their owners and feel so proud of themselves whenever they accomplish a behaviour.

You will not use food forever in getting the dog to obey your com-

Your Rottweiler is what you make him. He can be a trained pet or an ill-behaved nuisance.

mands. Food is only used to teach new behaviours, and once the dog knows what you want when you give a specific command, you will wean him off of the food treats but still maintain the verbal praise. After all,

In order to teach your Rottweiler, you must make eye contact and hold his attention.

Dogs do not understand our language. They can be trained to react to a certain sound, at a certain volume. If you say 'No, Oliver' in a very soft pleasant voice it will not have the same meaning as 'No, Oliver!!' when you shout it as loud as you can. You should never use the dog's name during a reprimand, just the command NO!! Since dogs don't understand words, comics use dogs trained with opposite meanings to the world. Thus, when the comic commands his dog to SIT the dog will stand up; and vice versa.

you will always have your voice with you, but there will be many times when you have no food rewards yet you expect the dog to obey.

Your Rottweiler can easily be trained to sit.

TEACHING DOWN

Teaching the down exercise is easy when you understand how the dog perceives the down position, and it is very difficult when you do not. In addition, teaching the down exercise using the wrong method can sometimes make the dog develop such a fear of the down that he either runs away when you say 'down' or he attempts to bite the person who tries to force him down.

Start the HEEL training with your dog sitting close to your left leg before taking a step forward.

Have the dog sit close alongside your left leg, facing in the same direction as you are. Hold the lead in your left hand and a food treat in your right. Now place your left hand lightly on the top of the dog's shoulders where they meet above the spinal cord. Do not push down on the dog's shoulders; simply rest your left hand there so you can guide the dog to lie down close to your left leg rather than to swing away from your side when he drops.

Now place the food hand at the dog's nose, say 'Down' very softly (almost a whisper), and slowly lower the food hand to the dog's front feet.

When the food hand reaches the floor, begin moving it forward along the floor in front of the dog. Keep talking softly to the dog, saying things like, 'Do you want this treat? You can do this, good dog.' Your reassuring tone of voice will help calm the dog as he tries to follow the food hand in order to get the treat.

When the dog's elbows touch the floor, release the food and praise softly. Try to get the dog to maintain that down position for several seconds before you let him sit up again. The goal here is to get the dog to settle down and not feel threatened in the down position.

In teaching the DOWN, give the dog a treat when his elbows touch the grass.

TEACHING STAY

It is easy to teach the dog to stay in either a sit or a down position. Again, we use food and praise during the teaching process as we help the dog to understand exactly what it is that we are expecting him to do.

To teach the sit/stay, start with the dog sitting on your left side as before and hold the lead in your left hand. Have a food treat in your right hand and place your food hand at the dog's nose. Say 'Stay' and step out on your right foot to stand directly in front of the dog, toe to toe, as he licks and nibbles the treat. Be sure to keep his head facing upward to maintain the sit position. Count to five and then swing around to stand next to the dog again with him on your left. As soon as you get back to the original position, release the food and praise lavishly.

To teach the down/stay, do the down as previously described. As soon as the dog lies down, say 'Stay' and step out on your right foot just as you did in the sit/stay. Count to five and then return to

stand beside the dog with him on your left side. Release the treat and praise as always.

Within a week or ten days, you can begin to add a bit of distance between you and your dog when you leave him. When you do, use your left hand open with the palm facing the dog as a stay signal, much the same as the hand signal a police officer uses to stop traffic at an intersection. Hold the food treat in your

right hand as before, but this time the food is not touching the dog's nose. He will watch the food hand and quickly learn that he is going to get that treat as soon as you return to his side.

When you can stand 1 metre away from your dog for 30 seconds, you can then begin building time and distance in both stays. Eventually, the dog can be expected to remain in the stay position for prolonged periods of time until you return to him or call him to you. Always praise lavishly when he stays.

Use praise and patience to train your Rottweiler to STAY in the down position.

85

DID YOU KNOW?

Dogs are sensitive to their master's moods and emotions. Use your voice wisely when communicating with your dog. Never raise your voice at your dog unless you are angry and trying to correct him. 'Barking' at your dog can become as meaningless as 'dogspeak' is to you. Think before you bark!

TEACHING COME

If you make teaching 'Come' a fun experience, you should never have a 'student' that does not love the game or that fails to come when called. The secret, it seems, is never to teach the word 'Come.'

At times when an owner most wants his dog to come when called, the owner is likely upset or anxious and he allows these feelings to come through in the tone of his voice when he calls his dog. Hear-ing that desperation in his owner's voice, the dog fears the results of going to him and therefore either disobeys outright or runs in the opposite direction. The secret, therefore, is to teach the dog a game and, when you want him to come to you, simply play the game. It is practically a no-fail solution!

To begin, have several members of your family take a few food treats and each go into a different room in the house. Take turns call-ing the dog, and each person should celebrate the dog's finding him with a treat and lots of happy praise. When a person calls the dog, he is actually inviting the dog to find him and get a treat as a reward for 'winning.'

A few turns of the 'Where are you?' game and the dog will figure out that everyone is playing the game and that each person has a big celebration awaiting his suc-

Your Rott-weiler should always come to you when called.

A group demonstration given by some well-trained Rottweilers and their handlers.

cess at locating them. Once he learns to love the game, simply calling out 'Where are you?' will bring him running from wherever he is when he hears that all-important question.

The come command is recognised as one of the most important things to teach a dog, so it is interesting to note that there are trainers who work with thousands of dogs and never teach the actual word 'Come.' Yet these dogs will race to respond to a person who uses the dog's name followed by 'Where are you?' In one instance, for example, a woman has a 12-year-old companion dog who went blind, but who never fails to locate her owner when asked, 'Where are you?'

Children particularly love to play this game with their dogs. Children can hide in smaller places like a shower or bathtub, behind a bed or under a table. The dog needs to work a little bit harder to find these hiding places, but when he does he loves to celebrate with a treat and a tussle with a favourite youngster.

When calling the dog, do not say 'Come.' Say things like, 'Rover, where are you? See if you can find me! I have a cookie for you!' Keep up a constant line of chatter with coaxing sounds and frequent questions such as, 'Where are you?' The dog will learn to follow the sound of your voice to locate you and receive his reward.

TEACHING HEEL

Heeling means that the dog walks beside the owner without pulling. It takes time and patience on the owner's part to succeed at teaching the dog that he (the owner) will not proceed unless the dog is walking calmly beside him. Pulling out ahead on the lead is definitely not acceptable.

You may choose to attend a training school with your Rottweiler.

Begin with holding the lead in your left hand as the dog sits beside your left leg. Hold the loop end of the lead in your right hand but keep your left hand short on the lead so it keeps the dog in close next to you.

Say 'Heel' and step forward on your left foot. Keep the dog close to

Teaching your Rott- weiler to COME is absolutely necessary.

you and take three steps. Stop and have the dog sit next to you in what we now call the 'heel position.' Praise verbally, but do not touch the dog. Hesitate a moment and begin again with 'Heel,' taking three steps and stopping, at which point the dog is told to sit again.

Your goal here is to have the dog walk those three steps without pulling on the lead. When he will walk calmly beside you for three steps without pulling, increase the number of steps you take to five. When he will walk politely beside you while you take five steps, you can increase the length of your walk to ten steps. Keep increasing the length of your stroll until the dog will walk quietly beside you without pulling as long as you want him to heel. When you stop heeling, indicate to the dog that the exercise is over by verbally praising as you pet him and say 'OK, good dog.' The 'OK' is used as a release word meaning that the exercise is finished and the dog is free to relax.

If you are dealing with a dog who insists on pulling you around, simply 'put on your brakes' and stand your ground until the dog realises that the two of you are not going anywhere until he is beside you and moving at your pace, not his. It may take some time just standing there to convince the dog that you are the leader and you will be the one to decide on the direction and speed of your travel.

Each time the dog looks up at you or slows down to give a slack lead between the two of you, quietly praise

In training to HEEL, gradually increase the number of steps you can take with your Rottweiler without him pulling on the lead.

him and say, 'Good heel. Good dog.' Eventually, the dog will begin to respond and within a few days he will be walking politely beside you without pulling on the lead. At first, the training sessions should be kept short and very positive; soon the dog will be able to walk nicely with you for increasingly longer distances. Remember also to give the dog free time and the opportunity to run and play when you are done with heel practice.

WEANING OFF FOOD IN TRAINING

Food is used in training new behaviours, yet once the dog understands what behaviour goes with a specific command, it is time to start weaning him off

Occasionally, a dog and owner who have not attended formal classes have been able to earn entry-level titles by obtaining competition rules and regulations from a local kennel club and practising on their own to a degree of perfection. Obtaining the higher level titles, however, almost always requires extensive training under the tutelage of experienced instructors. In addition, the more difficult levels require more specialised equipment whereas the lower levels do not.

the food treats. At first, give a treat after each exercise. Then, start to give a treat only after every other exercise. Mix up the times when you offer a food

89

Never train your dog, puppy or adult, when you are mad or in a sour mood. Dogs are very sensitive to human feelings, especially anger, and if your dog senses that you are angry or upset, he will connect your anger with his training and learn to resent or fear his training sessions.

behaviours such as sit, down, heel, etc. The more advanced levels of competition include jumping, retrieving, scent discrimination and signal work. The advanced levels require a dog and owner to put a lot of time and effort into their training; the titles that can be earned at these levels of competition are very prestigious.

reward and the times when you only offer praise so that the dog will never know when he is going to receive both food and praise and when he is going to receive only praise. This is called a variable ratio reward system and it proves successful because there is always the chance that the owner will produce a treat, so the dog never stops trying for that reward. No matter what, ALWAYS give verbal praise.

You should be taking a walk with your dog accompanying you. It should never be a battle of who is walking whom.

OBEDIENCE CLASSES
As previously discussed, it is a good idea to enrol in an obedience class if one is available in your area. Many areas have dog clubs that offer basic obedience training as well as preparatory classes for obedience competition. There are also local dog trainers who offer similar classes.

At obedience trials, dogs can earn titles at various levels of competition. The beginning levels of competition include basic

OTHER ACTIVITIES FOR LIFE
Whether a dog is trained in the structured environment of a class or alone with his owner at home, there are many activities that can bring fun and rewards to both owner and dog once they have mastered basic control.

Teaching the dog to help out around the home, in the garden

or on the farm provides great satisfaction to both dog and owner. In addition, the dog's help makes life a little easier for his owner and raises his stature as a valued companion to his family. It helps give the dog a purpose; it helps to keep his mind occupied and provides an outlet for his energy.

Backpacking is an exciting and healthful activity that the dog can be taught without assistance from more than his owner. The exercise of walking and climbing is good for man and dog alike, and the bond that they develop together is priceless.

If you are interested in participating in organised competition with your Rottweiler, there are other activities other than obedience in which you and your dog can become involved. Agility is a popular and fun sport where dogs run through an obstacle course that includes various jumps, tunnels and other exercises to test the dog's speed and coordination. The owners often run through the course beside their dogs to give commands and to guide them through the course. Although competitive, the focus is on fun—it's fun to do and fun to watch, as well as great exercise.

As a Rottweiler owner, you have the opportunity to participate in Schutzhund competition if you choose. Schutzhund origi-

Once you have trained your Rottweiler to sit reliably, you can move on to more advanced commands.

nated as a test to determine the best quality Rottweilers to be used for breeding stock. It is now used as a way to evaluate working ability and temperament, and some Rottweiler owners choose to train and compete with their dogs in Schutzhund trials. There are three levels of Schutzhund, ScH I, ScH II and ScH III, each level being progressively more difficult to complete successfully. Each level consists of training, obedience and protection phases. Training for Schutzhund is intense and must be practised consistently to keep the dog keen. The experience of Schutzhund training is very rewarding for dog and owner, and the Rottweiler's tractability is well suited for this type of training.

MEDICAL PROBLEMS
MOST FREQUENTLY SEEN IN ROTTWEILERS

Condition	Age Affected	Cause	Area Affected
Acral Lick Dermatitis	Any age, males	Unknown	Legs
Aortic Stenosis	Young pups	Congenital	Heart
Degenerative Myelopathy	1 to 3 years	Hereditary	Spinal cord/brain
Elbow Dysplasia	4 to 7 mos	Congenital	Elbow joint
Gastric Dilatation (Bloat)	Older dogs	Swallowing air	Stomach
Hip Dysplasia	By 2 years	Congenital	Hip joint
Hypothyroidism	1 to 3 years	Lymphocytic thyroiditis	Endocrine system
Osteochondrosis	4 to 7 months	Improper nutrition/exercise	Cartilage
Progressive Retinal Atrophy	Any age	Hereditary	Retinal tissue/eyes
Retinal Dysplasia	Birth	Hereditary	Retina
Von Willebrand's Disease	Birth	Congenital	Blood

Health Care of
Your Rottweiler

Dogs, being mammals like human beings, suffer many of the same physical illnesses as people. They might even share many of the psychological problems. Since people usually know more about human diseases than canine maladies, many of the terms used in this chapter will be the familiar terms, not necessarily those used by veterinary surgeons. We'll still use the term X-RAY, instead of the more acceptable term RADIOGRAPH. We will also use the familiar term SYMPTOMS even though dogs don't have symptoms, dogs have CLINICAL SIGNS. SYMPTOMS, by the way, are verbal descriptions of the patient's feelings. Since dogs can't speak, we have to look for clinical signs...but we still use the term SYMPTOMS in this book.

As a general rule, medicine is PRACTISED. That term is not arbitrary. Medicine is an art. It is a constantly changing art as we learn more and more about genetics, electronic aids (like CAT scans) and opinions. There are many dog maladies, like canine hip dysplasia, which are not universally treated in the same manner. Some veterinary surgeons opt for surgery more often than others.

SELECTING A
VETERINARY SURGEON

Your selection of a veterinary surgeon should not be based upon personality (as most are) but upon their convenience to your home. You want a doctor who is close as you might have emergencies or multiple visits for treatments. You want a doctor who has services that you might require such as microchipping or grooming facilities, who makes sophisticated pet supplies available and who has a good reputation for ability and responsiveness. There is nothing more frustrating than having to wait a day or more to get a response from a veterinary surgeon.

All veterinary surgeons are licensed and their diplomas and/or

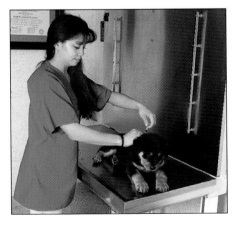

Select your veterinary surgeon based on proximity to your home and recommendations from other dog owners.

Your vet should give your Rottweiler puppy a thorough examination soon after you buy him.

certificates should be displayed in their waiting rooms. There are, however, many veterinary specialties which usually require further studies and internships. There are specialists in heart problems (veterinary cardiologists), skin problems (veterinary dermatologists), teeth and gum problems (veterinary dentists), eye problems (veterinary ophthalmologists), X-rays (veterinary radiologists), and surgeons who have specialties in bones, muscles or other organs. Most veterinary surgeons do routine surgery such as neutering, stitching up wounds and docking tails for those breeds in which such is required for show purposes. When the problem affecting your dog is serious, it is not unusual or impudent to get another medical opinion. You might also want to compare costs between several veterinary surgeons. Sophisticated health care and veterinary services can be very costly. Don't be bashful to discuss these costs with

An ounce of prevention is worth a pound of cure! Keep your dog healthy and visit the vet regularly.

94

your veterinary surgeon or his (her) staff. It is not infrequent that important decisions are based upon financial considerations.

PREVENTATIVE MEDICINE
It is much easier, less costly and more effective to practise preventative medicine than to fight bouts of illness and disease.

Properly bred puppies come from parents that were selected based upon their genetic disease profile. Their mothers should have

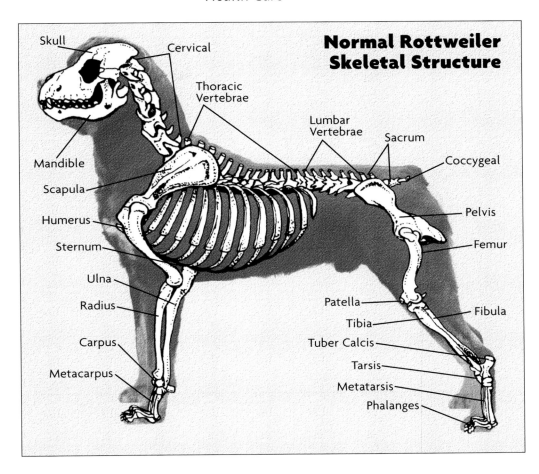

Normal Rottweiler Skeletal Structure

Skull
Cervical
Thoracic Vertebrae
Lumbar Vertebrae
Sacrum
Coccygeal
Mandible
Scapula
Humerus
Sternum
Ulna
Radius
Carpus
Metacarpus
Pelvis
Femur
Patella
Fibula
Tibia
Tuber Calcis
Tarsis
Metatarsis
Phalanges

been vaccinated, free of all internal and external parasites, and properly nourished. For these reasons, a visit to the veterinary surgeon who cared for the dam (mother) is recommended. The dam can pass on disease resistance to her puppies. This resistance can last for 8-10 weeks. She can also pass on parasites and many infections. That's why you should visit the veterinary surgeon who cared for the dam.

AFTER WEANING TO FIVE MONTHS OLD

Puppies should be weaned by the time they are about two months old. A puppy that remains for at least eight weeks with its mother and litter mates usually adapts better to other dogs and people later in its life.

In every case, you should have your newly acquired puppy examined by a veterinary surgeon immediately. Vaccination programmes usually begin when the puppy is very young.

The puppy will have its teeth examined, have its skeletal conformation checked, and have its general health checked prior to certification by the veterinary surgeon. Many puppies have problems with their knee caps, eye cataracts and other eye problems, heart murmurs and undescended testicles. They may also have personality problems and your veterinary surgeon might have training in temperament evaluation.

Your veterinary surgeon should schedule vaccinations. Keep a record yourself.

VACCINATION SCHEDULING

Most vaccinations are given by injection and should only be done by a veterinary surgeon. Both he and you should keep a record of the date of the injection, the identification of the vaccine and the amount given. The vaccination scheduling is based on a 15-day cycle. The first vaccinations should start when the puppy is 6-8 weeks old, then 15 days later when it is 10-12 weeks of age and later when it is 14-16 weeks of age. Vaccinations should NEVER be given without a 15-day lapse between injections. Most vaccinations immunise your puppy against viruses.

The usual vaccines contain immunising doses of several different

DID YOU KNOW?
Ridding your puppy of worms is VERY IMPORTANT because certain worms that puppies carry can infect humans, such as tapeworms, hookworms and roundworms.

Since puppies are never housebroken at two to three weeks of age, it is easy for them to pass on the parasites (worms) to humans.

Breeders initiate a deworming programme two weeks after weaning. The routine is repeated every two or three weeks until the puppy is three months old. The breeder from whom you obtained your Rottweiler puppy should provide you with the complete details of the deworming programme.

Your veterinary surgeon can prescribe and monitor the programme of deworming for you. The usual programme is treating the puppy every 15-20 days until the puppy is positively worm free.

It is not advised that you treat your puppy with drugs which are not recommended professionally.

viruses such as distemper, parvovirus, parainfluenza and hepatitis. There are other vaccines available when the puppy is at risk. You should rely upon professional advice. This is especially true for the booster shot programme. Most vaccination programmes require a booster when the puppy is a year old, and once a year thereafter. In some cases, circumstances may require more frequent immunisations.

HEALTH AND VACCINATION SCHEDULE

AGE IN WEEKS:	3RD	6TH	8TH	10TH	12TH	14TH	16TH	20-24TH
Worm Control	✔	✔	✔	✔	✔	✔	✔	✔
Neutering								✔
Heartworm		✔						✔
Parvovirus		✔		✔		✔		✔
Distemper			✔		✔		✔	
Hepatitis			✔		✔		✔	
Leptospirosis		✔		✔		✔		
Parainfluenza		✔		✔		✔		
Dental Examination			✔					✔
Complete Physical			✔					✔
Temperament Testing			✔					
Coronavirus					✔			
Kennel Cough		✔						
Hip Dysplasia							✔	
Rabies								✔

Vaccinations are not instantly effective. It takes about two weeks for the dog's immunisation system to develop antibodies. Most vaccinations require annual booster shots. Your veterinary surgeon should guide you in this regard.

Kennel cough, more formally known as *tracheobronchitis*, is treated with a vaccine which is sprayed into the dog's nostrils.

The effectiveness of a parvovirus vaccination programme can be tested to be certain that the vaccinations are protective. Your veterinary surgeon will explain and manage all of these details.

FIVE MONTHS TO ONE YEAR OF AGE

By the time your puppy is five months old, he should have completed his vaccination programme. During his physical examination he should be evaluated for the common hip dysplasia plus other diseases of

DID YOU KNOW?
Caring for the puppy starts before the puppy is born by keeping the dam healthy and well-nourished. When the puppy is about three weeks old, it must start its disease-control regimen. The first treatments will be for worms. Most puppies have worms, even if they are tested negative for worms. The test essentially is checking the stool specimens for the eggs of the worms. The worms continually shed eggs except during their dormant stage when they just rest in the tissues of the puppy. During this stage they don't shed eggs and are not evident during a routine examination.

the joints. There are tests to assist in the prediction of these problems. Other tests can also be run, such as the parvovirus antibody titer, which can assess the effectiveness of the vaccination programme.

Skin problems can be caused by contact with chemicals or other irritants.

Unless you intend to breed or show your dog, neutering the puppy at six months of age is recommended. Discuss this with your veterinary surgeon.

By the time your Rottweiler is seven or eight months of age, he can be seriously evaluated for his conformation to the club standard, thus determining his show potential and his desirability as a sire (or a dam). If the puppy is not top class and therefore is not a candidate for a serious breeding programme, most professionals advise neutering the puppy. Neutering has proven to be extremely beneficial to both male and female puppies. Besides the obvious impossibility of pregnancy, it inhibits (but does not prevent) breast cancer in bitches and prostate cancer in male dogs.

Blood tests are performed for heartworm infestation and it is possible that your puppy will be placed on a preventative therapy which will prevent heartworm infection as well as control other internal parasites.

DID YOU KNOW?

As Rottweiler puppies become more and more expensive, especially those puppies of high quality for showing and/or breeding, they have a greater chance of being stolen. The usual collar dog tag is, of course, easily removed. But there are two techniques which are becoming widely utilised for identification.

The puppy microchip implantation involves the injection of a small microchip, about the size of a corn kernel, under the skin of the dog. If your dog shows up at a clinic or shelter, or is offered for resale under less than savory circumstances, it can be positively identified by the microchip. The microchip is scanned and a registry quickly identifies you as the owner. This is not only protection against theft, but should the dog run away or go chasing a varmint and get lost, you have a fair chance of getting it back.

Tattooing is done on various parts of the dog, from its belly to its cheeks. The number tattooed can be your telephone number or any other number which you can easily memorise. When professional dog thieves see a tattooed dog, they usually lose interest in it. Both microchipping and tattooing can be done at your local veterinary clinic. For the safety of our Rottweilers, no laboratory facility or dog broker will accept a tattooed dog as stock.

DID YOU KNOW?

A dental examination is in order when the dog is between six months and one year of age and any permanent teeth that have erupted incorrectly can be corrected. It is important to begin a brushing regimen, preferably using a two-sided brushing technique, whereby both sides of the tooth are brushed at the same time. Durable nylon and safe edible chews should be a part of your puppy's arsenal for good health, good teeth and pleasant breath. The vast majority of dogs three to four years old and older has diseases of their gums from lack of dental attention. Using the various types of dental chews can be very effective in controlling dental plaque.

By the time your dog is a year old, you should have become very comfortable with your local veterinary surgeon and have agreed on scheduled visits for booster vaccinations. Blood tests should now be taken regularly, for comparative purposes, for such variables as cholesterol and triglyceride levels, thyroid hormones, liver enzymes, blood cell counts, etc.

The eyes, ears, nose and throat should be examined regularly and annual cleaning of the teeth is a ritual. For teeth scaling, the dog must be anaesthetised.

DOGS OLDER THAN ONE YEAR

Continue to visit the veterinary surgeon at least once a year. There is no such disease as old age, but bodily functions do change with age, and the eyes and ears are no longer as efficient. Neither are the internal workings of the liver, kidneys and intestines. Proper dietary changes, recommended by your veterinary surgeon, can make life more pleasant for the aging Rottweiler and you.

SKIN PROBLEMS IN ROTTWEILERS

Veterinary surgeons are consulted by dog owners for skin problems more than any other group of diseases or maladies. Dogs' skin is almost as sensitive as human skin and both suffer almost the same ailments. (Though the occurrence of acne in dogs is rare!) For this reason, veterinary dermatology has developed into a specialty practiced by many veterinary surgeons.

Some skin problems require the help of a veterinary dermatologist.

Since many skin problems have visual symptoms which are almost identical, it requires the skill of an experienced veterinary dermatologist to identify and cure many of the more severe skin disorders. Simply put, if your dog is suffering from a

99

skin disorder, seek professional assistance as quickly as possible. As with all diseases, the earlier a problem is identified and treated, the more successful is the cure.

HEREDITARY SKIN DISORDERS

Veterinary dermatologists are currently researching a number of skin disorders that are believed to have an hereditary basis. These inherited diseases are transmitted by both parents, who appear (phenotypically) normal but have a recessive gene for the disease, meaning that they carry, but are not affected by, the disease. These diseases pose serious problems to

breeders because in some instances there are no methods of identifying carriers. Often the secondary diseases associated with these skin conditions are even more debilitating than the skin disorders themselves, including cancers and respiratory problems.

Among the hereditary skin disorders, for which the mode of inheritance is known, are acrodermatitis, cutaneous asthenia (Ehlers-Danlos syndrome), sebaceous adenitis, cyclic hematopoiesis, dermatomyositis, IgA deficiency, colour dilution alopaecia and nodular dermatofibrosis.

PARASITE BITES

Many of us are allergic to mosquito bites. The bites itch, erupt and may even become infected. Dogs have the same reaction to fleas, ticks and/or mites. When you feel the prick of the mosquito when it bites you, you have a chance to kill it with your hand. Unfortunately, when your dog is bitten by a flea, tick or mite, it can only scratch it away or bite it. By the time the dog has been bitten, the parasite has done some of its damage. It may also have laid eggs to cause further problems in the near future. The itching from parasite bites is probably due to the saliva injected into the site when the parasite sucks the dog's blood.

AUTO-IMMUNE SKIN CONDITIONS

Auto-immune skin conditions are commonly referred to as being

There are many parasiticides which can be used around your home and garden to control fleas.

• Natural pyrethrins can be used inside the house.

• Allethrin, bioallethrin, permethrin and resmethrin can also be used inside the house but permethrin has been used successfully outdoors, too.

• Carbaryl can be used indoors and outdoors.

• Propxur can be used indoors.

• Chlorpyrifos, diazinon and malathion can be used indoors or outdoors and it has an extended residual activity.

• Ivermectin is effective against many external and internal parasites including heartworms, roundworms, tapeworms, flukes, ticks and mites.

allergic to yourself. Allergies, though, usually result in inflammatory reactions to an outside stimulus. Auto-immune diseases cause serious damage to the tissues which are involved.

The best known auto-immune disease is lupus. It affects people as well as dogs. The symptoms are very variable and may affect the

Food intolerance is the inability of the dog to completely digest certain foods. Puppies which may have done very well on their mother's milk may not do well on cow's milk. The result of this food intolerance may be loose bowels, passing gas and stomach pains. These are the only obvious symptoms to food intolerance and that makes diagnosis difficult.

Disease	What is it?	What causes it?	Symptoms
Leptospirosis	Severe disease that affects the internal organs; can be spread to people.	A bacterium, which is often carried by rodents, that enters through mucous membranes and spreads quickly throughout the body.	Range from fever, vomiting and loss of appetite in less severe cases to shock, irreversible kidney damage and possibly death in most severe cases.
Rabies	Potentially deadly virus that infects warm-blooded mammals.	A bacterium, which is often carried by rodents, that enters through mucous membranes and spreads quickly throughout the body.	1st stage: dog exhibits change in behaviour, fear. 2nd stage: dog's behaviour becomes more aggressive. 3rd stage: loss of coordination, trouble with bodily functions.
Parvovirus	Highly contagious virus, potentially deadly.	Ingestion of the virus, which is usually spread through the faeces of infected dogs.	Most common: severe diarrhoea. Also vomiting, fatigue, lack of appetite.
Kennel cough	Contagious respiratory infection.	Combination of types of bacteria and virus. Most common: *Bordetella bronchiseptica* bacteria and parainfluenza virus.	Chronic cough.
Distemper	Disease primarily affecting respiratory and nervous system.	Virus that is related to the human measles virus.	Mild symptoms such as fever, lack of appetite and mucous secretion progress to evidence of brain damage, 'hard pad.'
Hepatitis	Virus primarily affecting the liver.	Canine adenovirus type I (CAV-1). Enters system when dog breathes in particles.	Lesser symptoms include listlessness, diarrhoea, vomiting. More severe symptoms include 'blue-eye' (clumps of virus in eye).
Coronavirus	Virus resulting in digestive problems.	Virus is spread through infected dog's faeces.	Stomach upset evidenced by lack of appetite, vomiting, diarrhoea.

When a Rottweiler tirelessly licks a hot spot until the hair and skin have been removed, it is called acral lick. The cause of this syndrome is unknown.

SIMULATED MEDICAL CONDITION FOR EDUCATIONAL PURPOSES ONLY

kidneys, bones, blood chemistry and skin. It can be fatal to both dogs and humans, though it is not thought to be transmissible. It is usually successfully treated with cortisone, prednisone or similar corticosteroid, but extensive use of these drugs can have harmful side effects.

ACRAL LICK GRANULOMA
Rottweilers and other dogs about the same size, have a very poorly understood syndrome called acral lick. The manifestation of the problem is the dog's tireless attack at a specific area of the body, almost always the legs. They lick so intensively that they remove the hair and skin leaving an ugly, large wound. There is no absolute cure, but corticosteroids are the most common treatment.

AIRBORNE ALLERGIES
An interesting allergy is pollen allergy. Humans have hay fever, rose fever and other fevers with which they suffer during the pollinating season. Many dogs suffer the same allergies. So when the pollen count is high, your dog might suffer. Don't expect them to sneeze and have runny noses like humans. Dogs react to pollen allergies the same way they react to fleas—they scratch and bite themselves. Rottweilers are very susceptible to airborne pollen allergies.

Dogs, like humans, can be tested for allergens. Discuss the testing with your veterinary dermatologist.

FOOD ALLERGIES
Dogs are allergic to many foods which are best-sellers and highly recommended by breeders and veterinary surgeons. Changing the brand of food that you buy may not eliminate the problem because the element of the food to which the dog is allergic may also be contained in the new brand.

Recognizing a food allergy is difficult. Humans vomit or have rashes when they eat a food to which they are allergic. Dogs neither vomit nor (usually) develop a rash. Instead they itch, scratch and bite, thus making the diagnosis extremely difficult. While pollen allergies and parasite bites are usually seasonal, food allergies are year-round problems.

TREATING FOOD PROBLEMS
Handling food allergies and food intolerance yourself is possible. Put

your dog on a diet which it has never had. Obviously if it has never eaten this new food it can't have been allergic or intolerant of it. Start with a single ingredient which is NOT in the dog's diet at the present time. Ingredients like chopped beef or fish are common in dog's diets, so try something more exotic like rabbit, pheasant or even just vegetables such as potatoes. Keep the dog on this diet (with no additives) for a month. If the symptoms of food allergy or intolerance disappear, chances are that you have defined the cause.

Don't think that the single ingredient cured the problem. You still must find a suitable diet and ascertain which ingredient in the old diet was objectionable. This is most easily done by adding ingredients to the new diet one at a time until the problem is solved. Let the dog stay on the modified diet for a month before you add another ingredient.

An alternative method is to carefully study the ingredients in the diet to which your dog is allergic or intolerant. Identify the main ingredient in this diet and eliminate the main ingredient by buying a different food which does not have that ingredient. Keep experimenting until the symptoms disappear after one month on the new diet.

EXTERNAL PARASITES

Of all the problems to which dogs are prone, none is more well known and frustrating than fleas. Fleas, which usually refers to fleas, ticks

and mites, are relatively simple to cure but difficult to prevent. The opposite is true for the parasites which are harboured inside the body. They are a bit more difficult to cure but they are easier to control.

S.E.M. BY DR. DENNIS KUNKEL, UNIVERSITY OF HAWAII.

An S.E.M. (scanning electron micrograph), magnified and computer coloured, of a dog flea, Ctenocephalides canis.

FLEAS

It is possible to control flea infestation but you have to understand the life cycle of a typical flea in order to control them. Basically fleas are a summertime problem and their effective treatment (destruction) is environmental. The problem is that there is no single flea control medicine (insecticide) which can be used in every flea infested area. To understand flea control you must apply suitable treatment to the weak link in the life cycle of the flea.

THE LIFE CYCLE OF A FLEA

Fleas are found in four forms: eggs, larvae, pupae and adults. You really need a low-power microscope or hand lens to identify a living flea's eggs, pupae or larva. They spend their whole lives on your Rottweiler unless

103

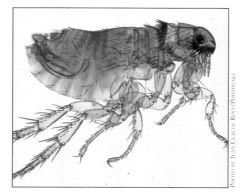

The magnified image of a male dog flea, Ctenocephalides canis.

PHOTO BY JEAN CLAUDE REVY/PHOTOTAKE

they are forcibly removed by brushing, bathing, scratching or biting.

Several species infest both dogs and cats. The dog flea is scientifically known as *Ctenocephalides canis* while the cat flea is *Ctenocephalides felis.* Cat fleas are very common on dogs.

Fleas lay eggs while they are in residence on your dog. These eggs do not adhere to the hair of your dog and they simply fall off almost as soon as they dry (they may be a bit damp when initially laid). These eggs are the reservoir of future flea infestations. If your dog scratches himself and is able to dislodge a few fleas,

Dog flea eggs magnified.

Male cat flea, Ctenocephalides felis, *commonly found on dogs as well as cats.*

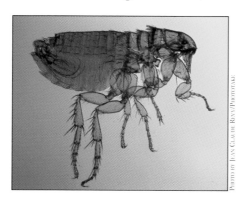

PHOTO BY JEAN CLAUDE REVY/PHOTOTAKE

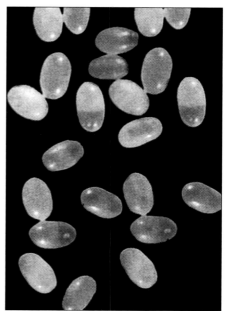

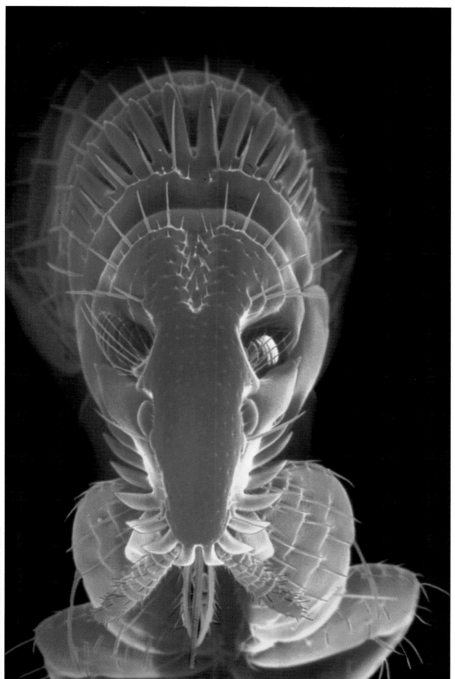

A scanning electron micrograph of a dog or cat flea, Ctenocephalides, *enlarged, magnified and coloured for effect.*

The Life Cycle of the Flea

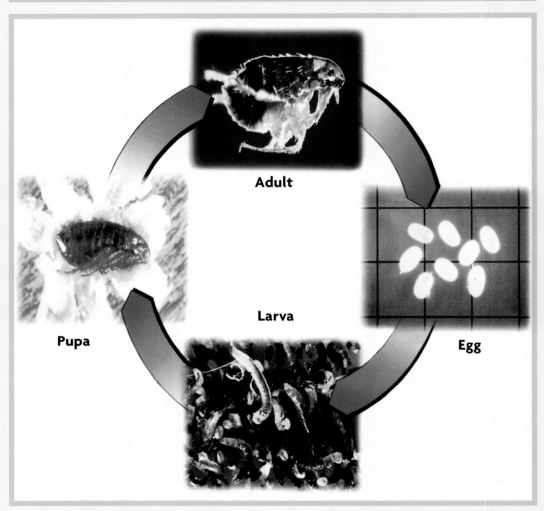

Adult

Egg

Larva

Pupa

The Life Cycle of the Flea was posterized by Fleabusters. Poster courtesy of Fleabusters®, Rx for Fleas.

PHOTO BY DWIGHT R. KUHN

flea larvae! All rugs and furniture must be vacuumed several times a day. Don't forget closets, under furniture, cushions. A study has reported that a vacuum cleaner with a beater bar can only remove 20% of the larvae and 50% of the eggs. The vacuum bags should be discarded into a sealed plastic bag or burned. The vacuum machine itself should be cleaned. The outdoor area to which your dog has access must also be treated with an insecticide.

Your vet will be able to recommend a household insecticidal spray,

An exceptional action photo showing a flea jumping from a dog's back.

Rottweilers can easily pick up fleas and ticks outdoors.

but this must be used with caution and instructions strictly adhered to.

While there are many drugs available to kill fleas on the dog itself, such as the miracle drug iver-

they simply fall off and await a future chance to attack a dog...or even a person. Yes, fleas from dogs bite people. That's why it is so important to control fleas both on the dog and in the dog's entire environment. You must, therefore, treat the dog and the environment simultaneously.

DE-FLEAING THE HOME
Cleanliness is the simple rule. If you have a cat living with your dog, the matter is more complicated since most dog fleas are actually cat fleas. But since cats climb onto many areas that are never accessible to dogs (like window sills, table tops, etc.), you have to clean all of these areas, too. The hard floor surfaces (tiles, wood, stone and linoleum) must be mopped several times a day. Drops of food onto the floor are actually food for

S.E.M. BY DR. DENNIS KUNKEL, UNIVERSITY OF HAWAII.

The head of the dog flea, Ctenocephalides canis, *magnified by a scanning electron micrograph.*

107

The dog tick, Dermacentor variabilis, *is the most common tick found on Rottweilers. Look at the eight legs! No wonder ticks are difficult to remove.*

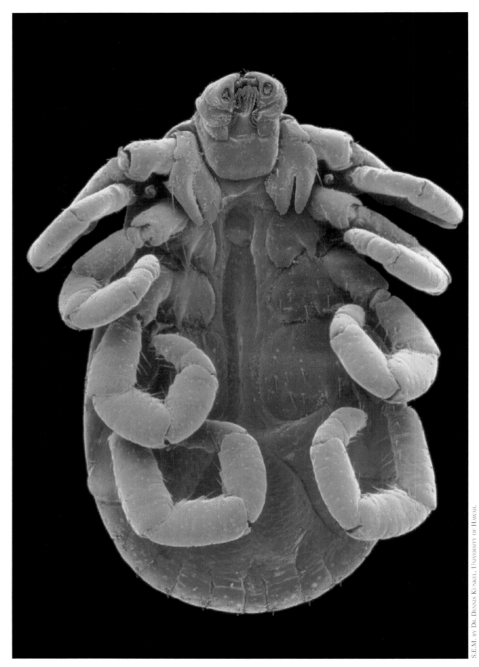

S.E.M. BY DR. DENNIS KUNKEL, UNIVERSITY OF HAWAII.

Photo by Dwight R. Kuhn

Your vet should be able to recommend a local service.

TICKS AND MITES

Though not as common as fleas, ticks and mites are found all over the tropical and temperate world. They don't bite, like fleas, rather they harpoon. They dig their sharp proboscis (nose) into the dog's skin and drink the blood. Their only food and drink is dog's blood. Dogs can get Lyme disease, Rocky Mountain spotted fever (normally found in the U.S. only), paralysis and many other diseases, from ticks and mites. They may live where fleas are found except they like to hide in cracks or seams in walls wherever dogs live. They are controlled the same way fleas are controlled.

The dog tick *Dermacentor variabilis* may well be the most com-

A photo of a human louse. It's very difficult to differentiate between lice from humans and lice from dogs.

mectin, it is best to have the de-fleaing and de-worming supervised by your vet. Ivermectin is effective against many external and internal parasites including heartworms, roundworms, tapeworms, flukes, ticks and mites. It has not been approved for use to control these pests, but veterinary surgeons frequently use it anyway. Ivermectin may not be available in all areas.

STERILISING THE ENVIRONMENT

Besides cleaning your home with vacuum cleaners and mops, you have to treat the outdoor range of your dog. This means trimming bushes, spreading insecticide and being careful not to poison areas in which fishes or other animals reside.

This is best done by an outside service specialising in de-fleaing.

Ticks can only live by ingesting blood.

mon dog tick in many geographical areas, especially those areas where the climate is hot and humid.

Most dog ticks have life expectancies of a week to six months, depending upon climatic conditions. They can neither jump nor fly, but they can crawl slowly and can range up to 5 metres (16 feet) to reach a sleeping or unsuspecting dog.

The mange mite, Psoroptes bovis, enlarged more than 200 times.

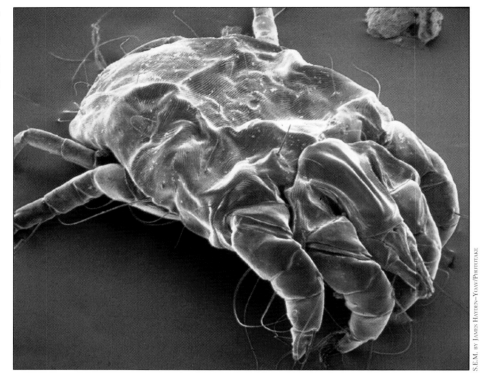

S.E.M. BY JAMES HAYDEN–YOAV/PHOTOTAKE

MANGE

Mites cause a skin irritation called mange. Some are contagious, like *Cheyletiella*, ear mites, scabies and chiggers. The non-contagious mites are *Demodex*. The most serious of the mites is the ear mite infestation. Ear mites are usually controlled with ivermectin.

It is essential that your dog be treated for mange as quickly as possible because some forms of mange are transmissible to people.

INTERNAL PARASITES

Most animals—fishes, birds and mammals, including dogs and humans—have worms and other parasites which live inside their bodies. According to Dr. Herbert R. Axelrod, the fish pathologist, there are two kinds of parasites: dumb and smart. The smart parasites live in peaceful cooperation with their hosts (symbiosis), while the dumb parasites kill their host. Most of the worm infections are relatively easy to control. If they are not controlled they eventually weaken the host dog to the point that other medical problems occur, but they are not dumb parasites.

ROUNDWORMS

The roundworms that infect dogs are scientifically known as *Toxocara canis*. They live in the dog's intestine. The worms shed eggs continually. It has been estimated that a Rottweiler produces about 150 grammes of faeces every day. Each gramme of faeces averages 10,000—12,000 eggs of roundworms. There are no known areas in which dogs roam that do not contain the eggs of roundworms. The greatest danger of roundworms is that they infect people, too! It is wise to have your dog tested regularly for roundworms.

The head of the dog tick, Dermacentor variabilis, *magnified and colourised.*

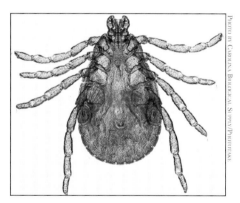

A brown dog tick, Rhipicephalus sanguineus.

Because it changes the site of its attachment about six times a day, the dog loses blood from each detachment, possibly causing iron-deficiency anaemia. They are easily purged from the dog with many medications, the best of which seems to be ivermectin even though it has not been approved for such use.

Pigs also have roundworm infections which can be passed to humans and dogs. The typical roundworm parasite is called *Ascaris lumbricoides*.

HOOKWORMS

The worm *Ancylostoma caninum* is commonly called the dog hookworm. It is dangerous to humans and cats. It also has teeth by which it attaches itself to the intestines of the dog.

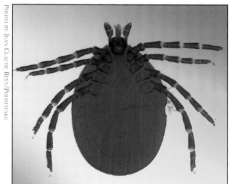

An uncommon dog tick of the genus Ixode, *magnified and colourised.*

Consider the following ways to arm yourself against fleas:
• Add a small amount of pennyroyal or eucalyptus oil to your dog's bath. These natural remedies repel fleas.
• Supplement your dog's food with fresh garlic (minced or grated) and a hearty amount of brewer's yeast, both of which ward off fleas.
• Use a flea comb on your dog daily. Submerge fleas in a cup of bleach to kill them quickly.
• Confine the dog to only a few rooms to limit the spread of fleas in the home.
• Vacuum daily...and get all of the crevices! Dispose of the bag every few days until the problem is under control.
• Cover cushions where your dog sleeps with towels, and wash the towels often
• Throw away your dog's flea collars. They are a waste of money and do not work!

TAPEWORMS

There are many species of tapeworms. They are carried by fleas! The dog eats the flea and thus starts the tapeworm cycle. Humans can also be infected with tapeworms, so don't eat fleas! Fleas are so small that your dog could pass them onto your hands, your plate or your food and thus make it possible for you to ingest a flea which is carrying tapeworm eggs.

While tapeworm infection is not life threatening in dogs (smart parasite!), it can be the cause of a very serious liver disease for humans. About 50 percent of the humans infected with *Echinococcus multilocularis*, causing alveolar hydatis, perish.

The round-worm, Ascaris lumbricoides, infects dogs and humans.

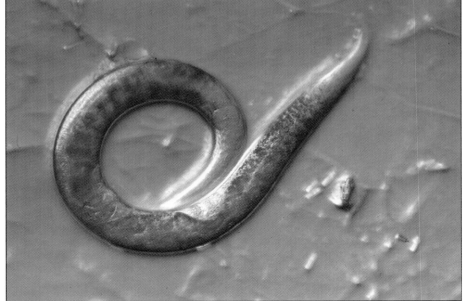

PHOTO BY CAROLINA BIOLOGICAL SUPPLY/PHOTOTAKE

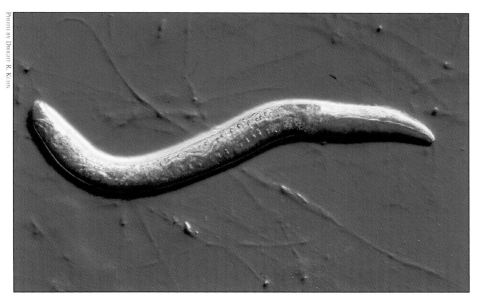

The round-worm, **Ascaris lumbricoides,** *infects humans, dogs and pigs.*

HEARTWORMS

Heartworms are thin, extended worms up to 30 cms (12 ins.) long which live in a dog's heart and major blood vessels around the heart. Rottweilers may have up to 200 of these worms. The symptoms may be loss of energy, loss of appetite, coughing, the development of a pot belly and anaemia.

Heartworms are transmitted by mosquitoes. The mosquito drinks the blood of an infected dog and takes in larvae with the blood. The larvae, called microfilaria, develop within the body of the mosquito and are passed on to the next dog bitten after the larvae mature. It takes two to three weeks for the larvae to develop to the infective stage within the body of the mosquito. Dogs should be

DID YOU KNOW?

Humans, rats, squirrels, foxes, coyotes, wolves, mixed breeds of dogs and purebred dogs are all susceptible to tapeworm infection. Except for humans, tapeworms are usually not a fatal infection. Infected individuals can harbour a thousand parasitic worms. Tapeworms have two sexes—male and female (many other worms have only one sex—male and female in the same worm). If dogs eat infected rats or mice, they get the tapeworm disease. One month after attaching to a dog's intestine, the worm starts shedding eggs. These eggs are infective immediately. Infective eggs can live for a few months without a host animal.

The roundworm, Rhabditis.

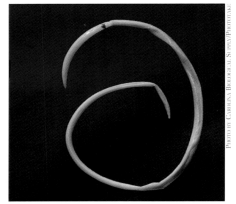

PHOTO BY CAROLINA BIOLOGICAL SUPPLY PHOTOTAKE

Male and female hookworms, Ancylostoma caninum, can infect Rottweilers.

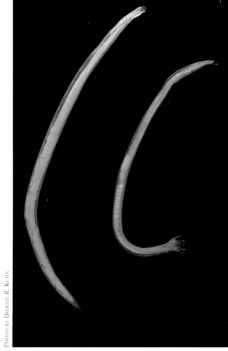

PHOTO BY DWIGHT R. KUHN

DID YOU KNOW?

Ivermectin is quickly becoming the drug of choice for treating many parasitic skin diseases in dogs.

For some unknown reason, herding dogs like Collies, Old English Sheepdogs, Australian Shepherds, etc., are extremely sensitive to ivermectin.

Ivermectin injections have killed some dogs, but dogs heavily infected with skin disorders may be treated anyway.

The ivermectin reaction is a toxicosis which causes tremors, loss of power to move their muscles, prolonged dilatation of the pupil of the eye, coma (unconsciousness), or cessation of breathing (death).

The toxicosis usually starts from 4-6 hours after ingestion (not injection), or as late as 12 hours. The longer it takes to set in, the milder is the reaction.

Ivermectin should only be prescribed and administered by a vet.

Some ivermectin treatments require two doses.

treated at about six weeks of age, then every six months.

Blood testing for heartworms is not necessarily indicative of how seriously your dog is infected. This is a dangerous disease. Dogs in the United Kingdom are not affected by heartworm.

DID YOU KNOW?

Don't let your dog drink from natural streams. The waterborne parasite *Giardia* causes severe diarrhoea—a sure way to spoil your tour of the great outdoors.

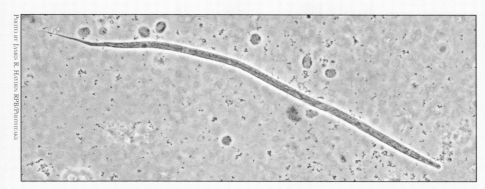

PHOTO BY JAMES R. HAYDEN RPB/PHOTOTAKE

The heart-worm, Dirofilaria immitis.

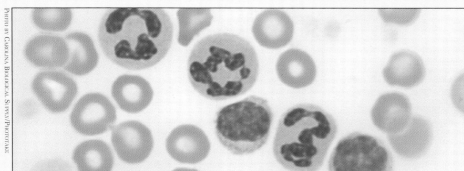

PHOTO BY CAROLINA BIOLOGICAL SUPPLY/PHOTOTAKE

Magnified heartworm larvae, Dirofilaria immitis.

PHOTO BY JAMES R. HAYDEN RPB/PHOTOTAKE

This surgically opened dog's heart is infected with canine heartworm, Dirofilaria immitis.

115

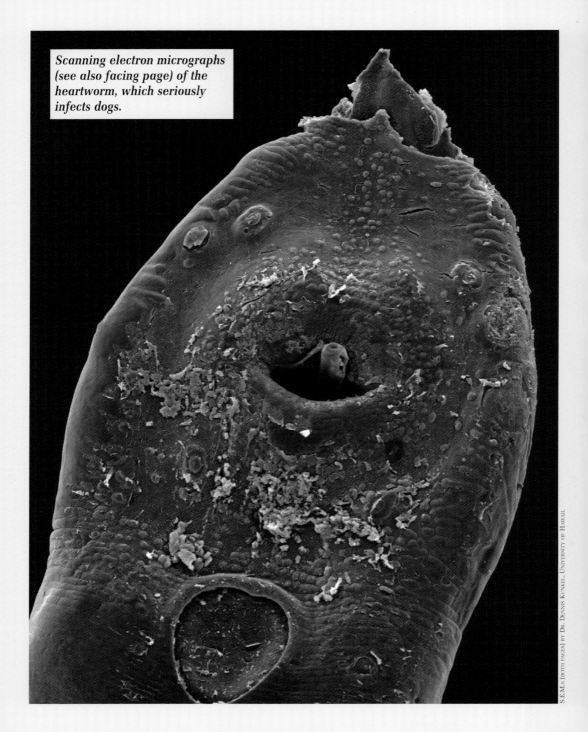

Scanning electron micrographs (see also facing page) of the heartworm, which seriously infects dogs.

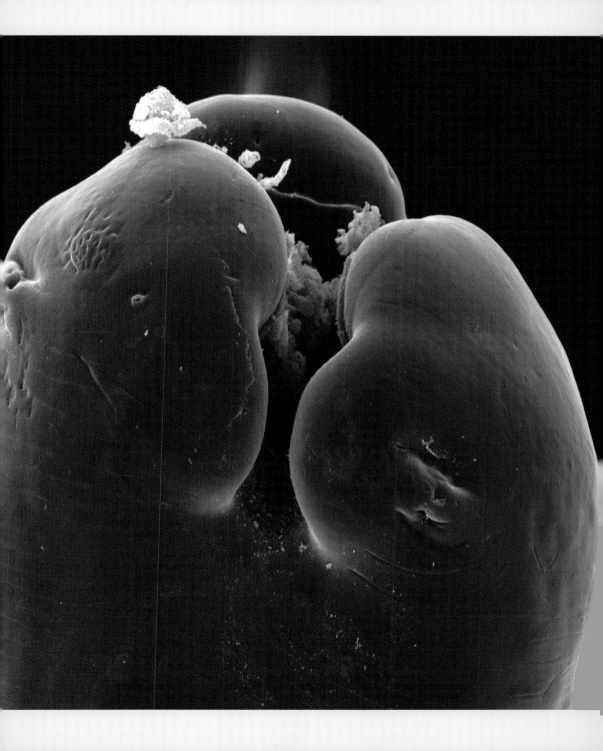

When your Rottweiler starts to slow down, rest a lot and stop running to greet you, you know your dog is getting old.

118

When Your Rottweiler Gets Old

The term old is a qualitative term. For dogs, as well as their masters, old is relative. Certainly we can all distinguish between a puppy Rottweiler and an adult Rottweiler—there are the obvious

physical traits such as size and appearance, and personality traits like their antics and the expressions on their faces. Puppies that are nasty are very rare. Puppies and young dogs like to play with children. Children's natural exuberance is a good match for the seemingly endless energy of young dogs. They like to run, jump, chase and retrieve. When dogs grow up and cease their interaction with children, they are often thought of as being too old to play with the kids.

The bottom line is simply that a dog is getting old when YOU think it is getting old because it slows down in its general activities, including walking, running, eating, jumping and retrieving. On the other hand, certain activities increase, like more sleeping, more licking your hands and body, more barking and more repetition of habits like going to the door when you put your coat on without being called.

On the other hand, if a Rottweiler is only exposed to people over 60 years of age, its life will normally be less active and it will not seem to be getting old as soon as its activity level slows down.

If people live to be 100 years old, dogs live to be 20 years old. While this is a good rule of thumb, it is VERY inaccurate. When trying

Don't make an old-timer bend to eat; raise the food bowl to his level.

to compare dog years to human years, you cannot make a generalisation about all dogs. You can make the generalisation that, say,

When the Rottweiler gets old, he will prefer to sit and await your arrival instead of jumping with joy the way he may previously have responded.

DID YOU KNOW?
An old dog starts to show one or more of the following symptoms:

• The hair on its face and paws starts to turn grey. The colour breakdown usually starts around the eyes and mouth.

• Sleep patterns are deeper and longer and the old dog is harder to awaken.

• Food intake diminishes.

• Responses to calls, whistles and other signals are ignored more and more.

• Eye contacts do not evoke tail wagging (assuming they once did).

nine years is a good life span for a Rottweiler, but you cannot compare it to that of a Chihuahua, as many small breeds typically live longer than large breeds. Dogs are generally considered mature within three years. They can reproduce even earlier. So the first three years of a dog's life are more like seven times that of comparable humans. That means a three-year-old dog is like a 21-year-old person. As the curve of comparison shows, there is no hard and fast rule for comparing dog and human ages. The comparison is made even more difficult, for not all humans age at the same rate...and human females live longer than human males.

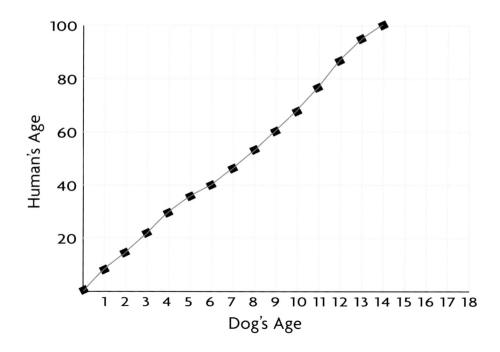

WHAT TO DO
WHEN THE TIME COMES

You are never fully prepared to make a rational decision about putting your dog to sleep. It is very obvious that you love your Rottweiler or you would not be reading this book. Putting a loved dog to sleep is extremely difficult. It is a decision that must be made with your veterinary surgeon. You are usually forced to make the decision when a life-threatening symptom becomes serious enough for you to seek medical (veterinary) help.

As your Rottweiler gets older, pay more attention during his routine dental care to check for tooth decay and gum disease.

The symptoms listed below are symptoms that gradually appear and become more noticeable. They are not life threatening, however, the symptoms below are to be taken very seriously and a discussion with your veterinary surgeon is warranted:

• Your dog cries and whimpers when it moves and stops running completely.

• Convulsions start or become more serious and frequent. The usual convulsion (spasm) is when the dog stiffens and starts to tremble being unable or unwilling to move. The seizure usually lasts for 5 to 30 minutes.

• Your dog drinks more water and urinates more frequently. Wetting and bowel accidents take place indoors without warning.

• Vomiting becomes more and more frequent.

If the prognosis of the malady indicates the end is near and your beloved pet will only suffer more and experience no enjoyment for the balance of its life, then there is no choice but euthanasia.

WHAT IS EUTHANASIA?

Euthanasia derives from the Greek meaning *good death*. In other words, it means the planned, painless killing of a dog suffering from a painful, incurable condition, or who is so aged that it cannot walk, see, eat or control its excretory functions.

Euthanasia is usually accomplished by injection with an overdose of an anaesthesia or barbiturate. Aside from the prick of the needle, the experience is painless.

HOW ABOUT YOU?

The days during which the dog becomes ill and the end occurs can be unusually stressful for you. If this is your first experience with the death of a loved one, you may need the comfort dictat-

The loss of a faithful and beloved pet is difficult to handle.

ed by your religious beliefs. If you are the head of the family and have children, you should have involved them in the decision of putting your Rottweiler to sleep. In any case, euthanasia alone is painful and stressful for the family of the dog. Unfortunately, it does not end there. The decision-making process is just as hard.

Older dogs won't be so eager to retrieve.

Usually your dog can be maintained on drugs for a few days while it is kept in the clinic in order to give you ample time to make a decision. During this time, talking with members of the family or religious representatives, or even people who have lived through this same experience, can ease the burden of your inevitable decision...but then what?

HOW ABOUT THE FINAL RESTING PLACE?

Dogs can have the same privileges as humans. They can be buried in their entirety in a pet cemetery (very expensive) in a burial container, buried in your garden in a place suitably marked with a stone or newly planted tree or bush, cremated with the ashes being given to you, or even stuffed and mounted by a taxidermist.

All of these options should be discussed frankly and openly with your veterinary surgeon. Do not be afraid to ask financial questions. Cremations are usually mass burning and the ashes you get may not be the ashes of your beloved dog.

There are very small crematoriums available to all veterinary clinics. If you want a private cremation, your vet can usually arrange it. However, this may be a little more expensive.

Some pet cemeteries have inexpensive sites in which you can store your deceased Rottweiler's ashes.

> **DID YOU KNOW?**
> The more open discussion you have about the whole stressful occurrence, the easier it will be for you when the time comes.

GETTING ANOTHER DOG?

The grief of losing your beloved dog will be as lasting as the grief of losing a human friend or relative. You cannot go out and buy another grandfather, but you can go out and buy another Rottweiler. In most cases, if your dog died of old age (if there is such a thing), it had slowed down considerably. Do you want a new Rottweiler puppy to replace it? Or are you better off in finding a more mature Rottweiler, say two to three years of age, which will usually be housetrained and will have an already developed personality.

Cemeteries for pets exist. Consult your veterinary surgeon to help you locate one.

If you decide that euthanasia is the right choice for your dog, it must be done by a licensed veterinary surgeon. There also may be societies for the prevention of cruelty to animals in your area. They often provide this service upon a vet's recommendation.

In this case, you can find out if you like each other after a few hours of being together.

The decision is, of course, your own. Do you want another Rottweiler? Perhaps you want a smaller or larger dog? How much do you want to spend on a dog? Look in your local newspapers for advertisements (*DOGS FOR SALE),* or, better yet, consult your local society for the prevention of cruelty to animals to adopt a dog. You may be able to find another Rottweiler, or you may choose another breed or a mixed-breed dog. It is harder to find puppies at an animal shelter, but there are often many adult dogs in need of new homes. Private dog kennels specialising in a particular breed are the source for high-quality dogs that they usually breed from champion stock.

Whatever you decide, do it as quickly as possible. Most people usually buy the same breed they had before because they know (and love) the characteristics of that breed. Then, too, they often know people who have the same breed and perhaps they are lucky enough that one of their friends expects a litter soon. What could be better?

More expensive burials can include engraved marble gravestones.

Showing Your Rottweiler

Is the Rottweiler puppy you selected growing into a handsome representative of his breed? You are rightly proud of your handsome little tyke, and he has mastered nearly all of the basic obedience commands that you have taught him. How about attending a dog show and seeing how the other half of the dog-loving world lives! Even if you never imagined yourself standing in the centre ring at the Crufts Dog Show, why not dream a little?

The first concept that the canine novice learns when watching a dog show is that each breed first competes against members of its own breed. Once the judge has selected the best member of each breed, then that chosen dog will compete with other dogs in its group. Finally the best of each group will compete for Best in Show and Reserve Best in Show.

The second concept that you must understand is that the dogs are not actually competing with one another. The judge compares each dog against the breed standard, which is a written description of the ideal specimen of the breed. This imaginary dog never walked into a show ring, has never been bred

Breeders attempt to get as close to the ideal as possible.

and, to the woe of dog breeders around the globe, does *not* exist. Breeders attempt to get as close to this ideal as possible, with every litter, but theoretically the 'perfect' dog is so elusive that it is impossible. (And if the 'perfect' dog were born, breeders and judges would never agree that it was indeed 'perfect.')

If you are interested in exploring dog shows, your best bet is to join your local breed club. These clubs host shows (often matches and open shows for beginners), send out newsletters, offer training days and pro

Dog show-ing is fun and educa-tional, and it can also be very rewarding.

vide an outlet to meet members who are often friendly and gener-ous with their advice and contacts. To locate the nearest breed club for you, contact The Kennel Club, the ruling body for the British dog world, not just for conformation shows, but for working trials, obe-dience trials, agility trials and field trials. The Kennel Club furnishes the rules and regulations for all these events plus general dog regis-tration and other basic require-ments of dog ownership. Its annual show, held in Birmingham, is the

WINNING THE TICKET

Earning a championship at Kennel Club shows is the most difficult in the world. Compared to the United States and Canada where it is rela-tively not 'challenging,' collecting three green tickets not only requires much time and effort, it can be very expensive! Challenge Certificates, as the tickets are properly known, are the building blocks of champions— good breeding, good handling, good training and good luck!

largest bench show in England. Every year no fewer than 20,000 of the U.K.'s best dogs qualify to par-ticipate in a marvelous show last-ing four days.

In shows held under the aus-pices of The Kennel Club, which includes Great Britain, Australia, South Africa and beyond, there are different kinds of shows. At the most competitive and presti-gious of these shows, the Champi-onship Shows, a dog can earn Challenge Certificates, and thereby become a 'champion.' A dog must earn three Challenge Certificates under three different judges to earn the prefix of 'Sh Ch' or 'Ch.' Note that some breeds must quali-fy in a field trial in order to gain the title of full champion. Chal-lenge Certificates are awarded to a very small percentage of the dogs competing, and the number of Challenge Certificates awarded in any one year is based upon the total number of dogs in each breed entered for competition. There are three types of Championship Shows: an all-breed General Championship show for all Ken-nel-Club-recognised; a Group Championship Show, limited to breeds within one of the groups; and a Breed Show, usually con-fined to a single breed.

Open Shows are generally less competitive and are fre-quently used as 'practice shows' for young dogs. These shows, of which there are hundreds each

You don't have to be an expert to get started in showing your Rottweiler. Every handler was a beginner at one time.

year, can be invitingly social events and are great first show experiences for the novice. If you're just considering watching a show to wet your paws, an Open Show is a great choice.

While Championship and Open Shows are most important for the beginner to understand, there are other types of shows in which the interested dog owner can participate. Training clubs, for example, sponsor Matches that can be entered on the day of the show for a nominal fee. These introductory level exhibitions are uniquely run: two dogs are pulled from a raffle and 'matched,' the winner of that match goes on to the next round, and eventually only one dog is left undefeated.

Exemption shows are similar in that they are simply fun classes and usually held in conjunction with small agricultural shows. Primary shows can also be entered on the day of the event and dogs entered must not have won anything towards their titles. Limited shows must be entered well in advance, and there are limitations upon who can enter. Beginners interested in showing their Rottweilers for the sake of experiencing the excitement of competing with others—and even taking home a ribbon or prize—should attend a Primary show. It is far better to begin at the simplest shows for the owner and dog alike. Regardless of which type show you choose to begin with, you and your dog will have a grand time competing and learning your way about the shows.

Before you actually step into the ring, you would be well advised to sit back and observe the judge's ring procedure. If it is your first time in the ring, do not be over-anxious and run to the front of the line. It is much better when you can stand back and study how the exhibitor in front of you is performing. The judge asks each handler to 'stand' the dog, hopefully showing the dog off to his best advantage. The judge

You should train your Rottweiler to stand so he will be well-behaved in front of a judge.

will observe the dog from a distance and from different angles, approach the dog, check his teeth, overall structure, alertness and muscle tone, as well as consider how well the dog 'conforms' to the standard. Most importantly, the judge will have the exhibitor move the dog around the ring in some

> **DID YOU KNOW?**
>
> Just like with anything else, there is a certain etiquette to the show ring that can only be learned through experience. Showing your dog can be quite intimidating to you as a novice when it seems as if everyone else knows what he's doing. You can familiarise yourself with ring procedure beforehand by taking a class to prepare you and your dog for conformation showing or by talking with an experienced handler. When you are in the ring, listen and pay attention to the judge and follow his/her directions. Remember, even the most skilled handlers had to start somewhere. Keep it up and you too will be a pro in no time!

pattern that he or she should specify (another advantage to not going first, but always listen since some judges change their directions, and the judge is always right!) Finally the judge will give the dog one last look before moving on to the next exhibitor.

If you are not in the top three at your first show, do not be discouraged. Be patient and consistent and you will eventually find yourself in the winning lineup. Remember that the winners were once in your shoes and have devoted many hours and much money to earn the placement. If you find that your dog is losing every time and never getting a nod, it may be time to consider a different dog sport or just to enjoy your Rottweiler as a pet.

WORKING TRIALS

Working trials can be entered by any well-trained dog of any breed, not just Gundogs or Working dogs. Many dogs that earn the Kennel Club Good Citizen Dog award choose to participate in a working trial. There are five stakes at both open and championship levels: Companion Dog (CD), Utility Dog (UD), Working Dog (WD), Tracking Dog (TD), and Patrol Dog (PD). Like in conformation shows, dogs compete against a standard and if the dog reaches the qualifying mark, it obtains a certificate. Divided into groups, each exercise must be achieved 70 percent in order to qualify. If the dog achieves 80 percent in the open level, it receives a Certificate of Merit (COM), in the championship level, it receives a Qualifying Certificate. At the CD stake, dogs must participate in four groups, Control, Stay, Agility and Search (Retrieve and Nosework). At the next three levels, UD, WD and TD, there are only three groups: Control, Agility and Nosework.

Agility consists of three jumps: a vertical scale, a six-foot wall of planks; a clear jump, a basic three-foot hurdle with a removable top bar; and a long jump of angled planks stretching nine feet.

To earn the UD, WD and TD, dogs must track approximately

Every part of the Rottweiler must be groomed for the show ring.

one-half mile for articles laid from one-half hour to three hours ago. Tracks consist of turns and legs, and fresh ground is used for each participant.

The fifth stake, PD, involves teaching manwork, which of course is not recommended for every breed.

An aspiring show dog starts training for the ring at an early age.

129

Champion Rottweilers do not necessarily make better pets than those that are not show quality... but what a joy when you can have both a great pet and a champion in the same dog!

Rottweilers can easily be trained for agility trials. It's fun for both dog and handler!

FIELD TRIALS AND WORKING TESTS

Working tests are frequently used to prepare dogs for field trials, the purpose of which is to heighten the instincts and natural abilities of gundogs. Live game is not used in working tests. Unlike field trials, working tests do not count toward a dog's record at the Kennel Club, though the same judges often oversee working tests. Field trials began in England in 1947, and are only moderately popular among dog folk. While breeders of Working and Gundog breeds concern themselves with the field abilities of their dogs, there is considerably less interest in field trials than dog shows. In order for dogs to become full champions, certain breeds must qualify in the field as well. Upon gaining three CCs in the show ring, the dog is designat-

At first you will have to manipulate your Rottweiler into the standing position, but after he is used to it he should assume the position on your command.

ed a Show Champion (Sh Ch). The title Champion (Ch) requires that the dog gain an award at a field trial, be a 'special qualifier' at a field trial or pass a 'special show dog qualifier' judged by a field trial judge on a shooting day.

AGILITY TRIALS

Agility trials began in the United Kingdom in 1977 and have since spread around the world, especially to the United States, where the sport enjoys strong popularity. The handler directs his dog over an obstacle course that includes jumps (such as those used in the working trials), as well as tyres, the dog walk, weave poles, pipe tunnels, collapsed tunnels, etc. The Kennel Club requires that dogs not be trained for agility until they are 12 months old. This dog sport intends to be great fun for dog and owner and interested own-

Practise with your Rottweiler as much as possible to be sure he becomes accustomed to standing politely. You don't want a restless dog when he is being gazed upon by a judge.

133

CLASSES AT DOG SHOWS

There can be as many as 18 classes per sex for your breed. Check the show schedule carefully to make sure that you have entered your dog in the appropriate class. Among the classes offered can be: Minor Puppy (ages 6 to 9 months); Puppy (ages 6 to 12 months); Junior (ages 6 to 18 months); Beginners (handler or dog never won first place); as well as the following, each of which is defined in the schedule: Maiden; Novice; Tyro; Debutant; Undergraduate; Graduate; Post-graduate; Minor Limit; Mid Limit; Limit; Open; Veteran; Stud Dog; Brood Bitch; Progeny; Brace; and Team.

Rottweilers at a dog show awaiting their turn in the ring.

ers should join a training club that has obstacles and experienced agility handlers who can introduce you and your dog to the 'ropes' (and tyres, tunnels and so on).

FÉDÉRATION CYNOLOGIQUE INTERNATIONALE

Established in 1911, the Fédération Cynologique Internationale represents the 'world kennel club,' the international body that brings uniformity to the breeding, judging and showing of purebred dogs. Although the FCI originally included only European

DID YOU KNOW?

You can get information about dog shows from kennel clubs and breed clubs:

Fédération Cynologique Internationale
14, rue Leopold II, B-6530 Thuin, Belgium

The Kennel Club
1-5 Clarges St., Piccadilly, London W1Y 8AB, UK
www.the-kennel-club.org.uk

American Kennel Club
5580 Centerview Dr., Raleigh, NC 27606-3390, USA
www.akc.org

Canadian Kennel Club
89 Skyway Ave., Suite 100, Etobicoke, Ontario
M9W 6R4 Canada
www.ckc.ca

Allgemeiner Deutscher Rottweiler Klub e.V. (ADRK)
Südring 18
32429 Minden, Germany
www.adrk.de

nations, namely France, Holland, Austria and Belgium, the latter of which remains the headquarters, the organisation today embraces nations on six continents and recognises well over 400 breeds of purebred dog. There are three titles attainable through the FCI: the International Champion, which is the most prestigious; the International Beauty Champion, which is based on aptitude certificates in different countries; and the International Trial Champion, which is based on achievement in obedience trials in different countries. Of course, quarantine laws in England and Australia prohibit most exhibitors from entering FCI shows, though the rest of the European Union do participate in these impressive canine spectacles, the largest of which is the World Dog Show, hosted in a different country each year. FCI sponsors both national and international shows. The hosting country determines the judging system and breed standards are always based on the breed's country of origin.

HOW TO ENTER A DOG SHOW

1. Obtain an entry form and show schedule from the Show Secretary.
2. Select the classes that you want to enter and complete the entry form.
3. Transfer your dog into your name at The Kennel Club. (Be sure that this matter is handled before entering.)
4. Find out how far in advance show entries must be made. Oftentimes it's more than a couple of months.

Winning! How sweet it is!!!

Recognising what your Rottweiler is trying to tell you is tantamount to being able to live harmoniously with your dog.

Understanding Your Dog's Behaviour

As a Rottweiler owner, you have selected your dog so that you and your loved ones can have a companion, a protector, a friend and a four-legged family member. You invest time, money and effort to care for and train the family's new charge. Of course, this chosen canine behaves perfectly! Well, perfectly like a dog.

THINK LIKE A DOG

Dogs do not think like humans, nor do humans think like dogs, though we try. Unfortunately, a dog is incapable of figuring out how humans think, so the responsibility falls on the owner to adopt a proper canine mindset. Dogs cannot rationalise, and dogs exist in the present moment. Many dog owners make the mistake in training of thinking that they can reprimand their dog for something he did a while ago. Basically, you cannot even reprimand a dog for something he did 20 seconds ago! Either catch him in the act or for-

A dam with her puppies will act very protectively. Think of how a human mother might protect her child.

Since you'll be checking your Rottweiler's ears regularly, train the dog when he is a puppy to tolerate your inspections.

get it! It is a waste of your and your dog's time—in his mind, you are reprimanding him for whatever he is doing at that moment.

The following behavioural problems represent some which owners most commonly encounter. Every dog is unique and every situation is unique. No author could purport to solve your Rottweiler's problem simply by reading a script. Here we outline some basic 'dogspeak' so that owners' chances of solving behavioural problems are increased. Discuss bad habits with your veterinary surgeon and he/she can recommend a behavioural specialist to consult in appropriate cases. Since behavioural abnormalities are the leading reason owners abandon their pets, we hope that you will make a valiant effort to solve your Rottweiler's problem. Patience and understanding are virtues that dwell in every pet-loving household.

By starting to examine your Rottweiler's teeth at an early age, you'll be able to examine his teeth with no problem when he gets older.

AGGRESSION

Aggression can be a very big problem in dogs, especially big dogs. Aggression, when not controlled, becomes dangerous. An aggressive dog, no matter the size, may lunge at, bite or even attack a person or another dog. Aggressive behaviour is not to be tolerated. It is more than just inappropriate behaviour; it is not safe, especially with a large, powerful breed such as the Rottweiler. It is painful for a family to watch their dog become unpredictable in his behaviour to the point where they are afraid of the dog. And while not all aggressive behaviour is dangerous, it can be frightening: growling, baring teeth, etc. It is important to get to the root of the problem to ascertain why the dog is acting in this manner. Aggression is a display of dominance, and the dog should not have the dominant role in its pack, which is, in this case, your family.

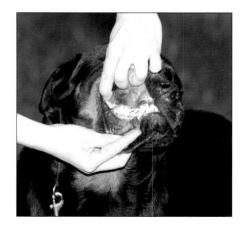

No matter how friendly a dog appears, always approach a strange dog with caution and ask the owner's permission before petting the dog.

It is important not to challenge an aggressive dog as this could provoke an attack. Observe your Rottweiler's body language. Does he make direct eye contact and stare? Does he try to make himself as large as possible: ears pricked, chest out, tail erect? Height and size signify authority in a dog pack—being taller or 'above' another dog literally means that he is 'above' in the social status. These body signals tell you that your Rottweiler thinks he is in charge, a problem that needs to be dealt with. An aggressive dog is unpredictable in that you never know when he is going to strike and what he is going to do. You cannot understand why a dog that is playful and loving one minute is growling and snapping the next.

The best solution is to consult a behavioural specialist, one who has experience with the Rottweiler if possible. Together, perhaps you can pinpoint the cause of your dog's aggression and do something about it. An aggressive

139

Rottweilers must be exposed to other dogs when they are young so they will tolerate them when they are older.

dog cannot be trusted, and a dog that cannot be trusted is not safe to have as a family pet. If the pet Rottweiler becomes untrustworthy, he cannot be kept in the home with the family. The family must get rid of the dog. In the worst case, the dog must be euthanised.

AGGRESSION TOWARD OTHER DOGS
A dog's aggressive behaviour toward another dog stems from

When a Rottweiler bares his teeth, be careful. In this case, though, the dog's expression looks more like a smile than a display of aggression...yes, dogs can smile.

not enough exposure to other dogs at an early age. If other dogs make your Rottweiler nervous and agitated, he will lash out as a protective mechanism. A dog who has not received sufficient exposure to other canines tends to believe that

Dogs of all breeds can get along. Most dogs that grow up together become very accustomed to one another.

140

This Rottweiler looks out to see what is going on. Her puppy is outside and, thus, she responds in a protective manner.

Older dogs and puppies bond easily even if the puppy is not the dam's.

he is the only dog on the planet. The animal becomes so dominant that he does not even show signs that he is fearful or threatened. Without growling or any other physical signal as a warning, he will lunge at and bite the other dog. A way to correct this is to let your Rottweiler approach another dog when walking on lead. Watch very closely and at the very first sign of aggression, correct your

Rottweiler and pull him away. Scold him for any sign of discomfort, and then praise him when he ignores or tolerates the other dog. Keep this up until either he stops the aggressive behaviour, learns to ignore the other dog or even accepts other dogs. Praise him lavishly for his correct behaviour.

DOMINANT AGGRESSION
A social hierarchy is firmly established in a wild dog pack. The dog wants to dominate those under him and please those above him. Dogs know that there must be a leader. If you are not the obvious choice for emperor, the dog will assume the throne! These conflicting innate desires are what a dog owner is up against when he sets about training a dog. In training a dog to obey commands, the

Multiple-dog households are very common and usually pose no problems to the owner. These two live together and seem completely oblivious of each other's existence.

owner is reinforcing that he is the top dog in the 'pack' and that the dog should, and should want to, serve his superior. Thus, the owner is suppressing the dog's urge to dominate by modifying his behaviour and making him obedient.

An important part of training is taking every opportunity to reinforce that you are the leader. The simple action of making your Rottweiler sit to wait for his food instead of allowing him to run up to get it when he wants it says that you control when he eats; he is dependent on you for food. Although it may be difficult, do not give in to your dog's wishes every time he whines at you or looks at you with pleading eyes. It is a constant effort to show the dog that

his place in the pack is at the bottom. This is not meant to sound cruel or inhumane. You love your Rottweiler and you should treat him with care and affection. You (hopefully) did not get a dog just so you could boss around another creature. Dog training is not about being cruel or feeling important, it is about moulding the dog's behaviour into what is acceptable and teaching him to live by your rules. In theory, it is quite simple: catch him in appropriate behaviour and reward him for it. Add a dog into the equation and it becomes a bit more trying, but as a rule of thumb, positive reinforcement is what works best.

With a dominant dog, punishment and negative reinforcement can have the opposite effect of what you are after. It

Fear in a grown dog is often the result of improper or incomplete socialisation as a pup, or it can be the result of a traumatic experience he suffered when young. Keep in mind that the term 'traumatic' is relative—something that you would not think twice about can leave a lasting negative impression on a puppy. If the dog experiences a similar experience later in life, he may try to fight back to protect himself. Again, this behaviour is very unpredictable, especially if you do not know what is triggering his fear.

When a Rottweiler growls and bares his teeth with his mouth slightly agape, you should be careful. This might be the sign of an aggressive dog.

Never let a Rottweiler think he is in control. If you develop a dominant dog, you will probably need a trainer's help to correct the situation.

can make a dog fearful and/or act out aggressively if he feels he is being challenged. Remember, a dominant dog perceives himself at the top of the social heap, and will fight to defend his perceived status. The best way to prevent that is to never give him reason to think that he is in control in the first place. If you are having trouble training your Rottweiler and it seems as if he is constantly challenging your authority, seek the help of an obedience trainer or behavioural specialist. A professional will work with both you and your dog to teach you effective techniques to use at home. Beware of trainers who rely on excessively harsh methods; scolding is necessary

now and then, but the focus in your training should always be on positive reinforcement.

If you can isolate what brings out the fear reaction, you can help the dog get over it. Supervise your Rottweiler's interactions with people and other dogs, and praise the dog when it goes well. If he starts to act aggressively in a situation, correct him and remove him from the situation. Do not let people approach the dog and start petting him without your express permission. That way, you can have the dog sit to accept petting, and praise him when he behaves properly. You are focusing on praise and on modifying his behaviour by rewarding him when he acts appropriately. By being gentle and by supervising his interactions, you are showing him that there is no need to be afraid or defensive.

We all love our dogs and our dogs love us. They show their love and affection by licking us. This is not a very sanitary practice as dogs lick and sniff in some unsavory places. Kissing your dog on the mouth is strictly forbidden, as parasites can be transmitted in this manner.

SEXUAL BEHAVIOUR

Dogs exhibit certain sexual behaviours that may have influenced your choice of male or female when you first purchased your Rottweiler. Spaying/neutering will eliminate these behaviours, but if you are purchasing a dog that you wish to breed, you should be aware of what you will have to deal with throughout the dog's life.

Owners must further recognise that mounting is not merely a sexual expression but also one of dominance. Be consistent and persistent and you will find that you can 'move mounters.'

CHEWING

The national canine pastime is chewing! Every dog loves to sink his 'canines' into a tasty bone, but sometimes that bone

Rottweilers that get enough exercise are less prone to destructive behaviour.

Female dogs usually have two oestruses per year, each season lasting about three weeks. These are the only times in which a female dog will mate, and she usually will not allow this until the second week of the cycle. If a bitch is not bred during the heat cycle, it is not uncommon for her to experience a false pregnancy, in which her mammary glands swell and she exhibits maternal tendencies toward toys or other objects.

is attached to his owner's hand! Dogs need to chew, to massage their gums, to make their new teeth feel better and to exercise their jaws. This is a natural behaviour deeply imbedded in all things canine. Our role as owners is not to stop chewing, but to redirect it to positive, chew-worthy objects. Be an informed owner and purchase proper chew toys for your Rottweiler, like strong nylon bones made for large

145

dogs. Be sure that the devices are safe and durable, since your dog's safety is at risk. Again, the owner is responsi-

Don't kiss your dog on the mouth. It is not sanitary.

ble for ensuring a dog-proof environment. The best answer is prevention: that is, put your shoes, handbags and other tasty objects in their proper places (out of the reach of the growing canine mouth). Direct puppies to their toys whenever you see them tasting the furniture legs or the leg of your trousers. Make a loud noise to attract the pup's attention and immediately escort him to his chew toy and engage him with the toy for at least four minutes, praising and encouraging him all the while.

Some trainers recommend deterrents, such as hot pepper or another bitter spice or a product designed for this purpose, to discourage the dog from chewing on unwanted objects. This is sometimes reliable, though not as often as the manufacturers of such products claim. Test out the product with your own dog before investing in a case of it.

Dogs need to chew... even if it is on your toes! Since puppies have needle-sharp teeth, they can inflict a painful (though playful) bite.

146

JUMPING UP

Jumping up is a dog's friendly way of saying hello! Some dog owners do not mind when their dog jumps up, which is fine for them. The problem arises when guests come to the house and the dog greets them in the same manner—whether they like it or not! However friendly the greeting may be, chances are your visitors will not appreciate nearly being knocked over by 50 kgs. of Rottweiler. The dog will not be able to distinguish upon whom he can jump and whom he cannot. Therefore, it is probably best to discourage this behaviour entirely.

Pick a command such as 'off' (avoid using 'down' since you will use that for the dog to lie down) and tell him 'off' when he jumps up. Place him on the ground on all fours and have him sit, praising him the whole time. Always lavish him with praise and petting when he is in the 'sit' position. That way you are still giving him a warm affectionate greeting, because you are as excited to see him as he is to see you!

DIGGING

Digging, which is seen as a destructive behaviour to humans, is actually quite a natural behaviour in dogs. Whether or not your dog is one of the 'earth dogs' (also known as terriers), his desire to dig can be irrepressible and most frustrating to his owners. When digging occurs in your garden, it is actually a normal behaviour redirected into something the dog can do in his everyday life. For example, in the wild a dog would be actively seeking food, making his own shelter, etc. He would be using his paws in a purposeful manner; he would be using them

for his survival. Since you provide him with food and shelter, he has no need to use his paws for these purposes, and so the energy that he would be using

Praise your pup when he behaves and responds to commands.

manifests itself in the form of little holes all over your garden and flower beds.

Perhaps your dog is digging as a reaction to boredom—it is somewhat similar to someone eating a whole bag of crisps in front of the television—because they are there and there is not anything better to do! Basically, the answer is to provide the dog with adequate play and exercise so that his mind and paws are occupied, and so that he feels as if he is doing something useful.

Of course, digging is easiest to control if it is stopped as soon as possible, but it is often hard to catch a dog in the act, especially if he is alone in the garden during the day. If your dog is a compulsive digger and is not easily distracted by other activities, you can designate an area on your property where it is okay for him to dig. If you catch him digging in an off-limits area of the garden, immediately bring him to the approved

DID YOU KNOW?

Males, whether whole or altered, will mount most anything: a pillow, your leg or, much to your horror, even your neighbour's leg. As with other types of inappropriate behaviour, the dog must be corrected while in the act, which for once is not difficult. Often he will not let go! While a puppy, experimenting with his very first urges, his owners feel he needs to 'sow his oats' and allow the pup to mount. As the pup grows into a full-size dog, with full-size urges, it becomes a nuisance and an embarrassment. Males always appear as if they are trying to 'save the race,' more determined and strong than imaginable. While altering the dog at an appropriate age will limit the dog's desire, it usually does not remove it entirely.

147

area and praise him for digging there. Keep a close eye on him so that you can catch him, as that is the only way he is going to understand what is permitted and what is not. If you bring him to a hole he dug an hour ago and tell him 'No,' he will understand that you are not fond of holes, or dirt, or flowers. If you catch him while he is stifle-deep in your tulips, that is when he will get your message.

Your dog can easily become your most loyal friend.

BARKING

Dogs cannot talk—oh, what they would say if they could! Instead, barking is a dog's way of 'talking.' It can be somewhat frustrating because it is not always easy to tell what a dog means by his bark—is he excited, happy, frightened, angry? Whatever it is that the dog is trying to say, he should not be punished for barking. It is only when the barking becomes excessive, and when the excessive barking becomes a bad habit, does the behaviour need to be modified. If an intruder came into your home in the middle of the night and the dog barked a warning, wouldn't you be pleased? You would probably deem your dog a hero, a wonderful guardian and protector of the home.

On the other hand, if a friend drops by unexpectedly and rings the doorbell and is greeted with a sudden sharp bark, you would probably be annoyed at the dog. But isn't it just the same behaviour? The dog does not know any better...unless he sees who is at the door and it is someone he is familiar with, he will bark as a means of vocalising that his (and your) territory is being threatened. While your friend is not posing a threat, it is all the same to the dog. Barking is his means of letting you know that there is an intrusion, whether friend or foe, on your property. This type of barking is instinctive and should not be discouraged.

Excessive habitual barking, however, is a problem that should be corrected early on. As your Rottweiler grows up, you will be able to tell when his barking is purposeful and when it is for no reason. You will become able to distinguish your dog's different barks and with what they are associated. For example, the bark when someone comes to the door will be different from the bark when he is excited to see you. It is similar to a person's tone of voice, except that the dog has to rely totally on tone of voice because he does not have the benefit of using words. An incessant barker will be evident at an early age.

There are some things that encourage a dog to bark. For example, if your dog barks non-stop for a few minutes and you give him a treat to quiet him, he believes that you are rewarding him for barking. He will associate barking with getting a treat, and will keep doing it until he is rewarded.

FOOD STEALING

Is your dog devising ways of stealing food from your counter tops? If so, you must answer the following questions: Is your Rottweiler hungry, or is he 'constantly famished' like every other chow hound? Why is there food on the counter top? Face it, some dogs are more food-motivated than others; some dogs are totally obsessed by a slab of brisket and can only think of their next meal. Food stealing is terrific fun and always yields a great reward— FOOD, glorious food.

The owner's goal, therefore, is to make the 'reward' less rewarding, even startling! Plant a shaker can (an empty pop can with coins inside) on the counter so that it catches your pooch offguard. There are other devices available that will surprise the dog when he is looking for a mid-afternoon snack. Such remote-control devices, though not the first choice of some trainers, allow the correction to come from the object instead of the owner. These devices are also useful to keep the snacking hound from napping on furniture that is forbidden.

BEGGING

Just like food stealing, begging is a favourite pastime of hungry puppies! With that same reward— FOOD! Dogs quickly learn that their owners keep the 'good food'

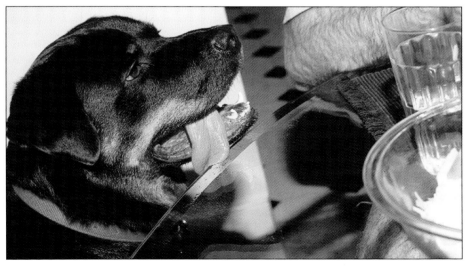

A dog that begs at the dinner table can be quite a nuisance. Once you start feeding your Rottweiler from the table, he will interpret this as being rewarded for his behaviour.

149

Never give in to a beggar. The only way to break the begging habit is to ignore it.

for themselves, and that we humans do not dine on kibble alone. Begging is a conditioned response related to a specific stimulus, time and place. The sounds of the kitchen, cans and bottles opening, crinkling bags, the smell of food in preparation, etc., will excite the chow hound and soon the paws are in the air!

Here is the solution to stopping this behaviour: Never give into a beggar! You are rewarding the dog for sitting pretty, jumping up, whining and rubbing his nose into you by giving him that glorious reward—food. By ignoring the dog, you will (eventually) force the behaviour into extinction. Note that the behaviour likely gets worse before it disappears, so be sure there are not any 'softies' in the family who will give in to little 'Oliver' every time he whimpers, 'More, please.'

SEPARATION ANXIETY

Puppies first experience separation anxiety, that is fear of being left alone, as soon as they are weaned and removed from their dam. This is a normal reaction, no different than the child who cries as his mum leaves him on the first day of school. Don't be like your sappy mum and cry right back—move on, and your Rottweiler puppy will suffer less in the long run.

Your Rottweiler may howl, whine or otherwise vocalise his displeasure at your leaving the house and his being left alone. This is a normal case of separation anxiety, but there are things that can be done to eliminate this problem. Your dog needs to learn that he will be fine on his own for a while and that he will not wither away if he is not attended to every minute of the day. In fact, constant attention

DID YOU KNOW?
Dogs and humans may be the only animals that smile. They imitate the smile on their owner's face when they greet each other. The dog only smiles at its human friends. It never smiles at another dog or cat. Usually it rolls up its lips and shows its teeth in a clenched mouth while it rolls over onto its back begging for a soft scratch.

can lead to separation anxiety in the first place. If you are endlessly coddling and cooing over your dog, he will come to expect this from you all of the time and it will be more traumatic for him when you are not there. Obviously, you enjoy spending time with your dog, and he thrives on your love and attention. However, it should not become a dependent relationship where he is heartbroken without you.

One thing you can do to minimise separation anxiety is to make your entrances and exits as low-key as possible. Do not give your dog a long drawn-out goodbye, and do not lavish him with hugs and kisses when you return. This is giving in to the attention that he craves, and it will only make him miss it more when you are away. Another thing you can try is to give your dog a treat when you

Leaving your pup alone can be easier if he has a familiar toy to keep him company when you are not with him.

leave; this will not only keep him occupied and keep his mind off the fact that you just left, but it will also help him associate your leaving with a pleasant experience.

You may have to accustom your dog to being left alone in intervals, much like when you introduced your pup to his crate. Of course, when your dog starts whimpering as you approach the door, your first instinct will be to run to him and comfort him, but do not do it! Really—eventually he will adjust and be just fine if you take it in small steps. His anxiety stems from being placed in an unfamiliar situation; by familiarising him with being alone he will learn that he is okay. That is not to say you should purposely leave your dog home alone, but the dog needs to know that while he can depend on you for his care, you do not have to be by his side 24 hours a day.

When the dog is alone in the house, he should be confined to his crate or a designated dog-proof area of the house. This should be the area in which he sleeps, so he

DID YOU KNOW?

The number of dogs who suffer from separation anxiety is on the rise as more and more pet owners find themselves at work all day. New attention is being paid to this problem, which is especially hard to diagnose since it is only evident when the dog is alone. Research is currently being done to help educate dog owners about separation anxiety and about how they can help minimise this problem in their dogs.

should already feel comfortable there and this should make him feel more at ease when he is alone. This is just one of the many examples in which a crate is an invaluable tool for you and your dog, and another reinforcement of why your dog should view his crate as a 'happy' place, a place of his own.

COPROPHAGIA
Faeces eating is, to most humans, one of the most disgusting behaviours that their dog could engage in, yet to the dog it is perfectly normal. It is hard for us to understand why a dog would want to eat its own faeces; he could be seeking certain nutrients that are missing from his diet, he could be just plain hungry, or he could be attracted by the pleasing (to a dog) scent. While coprophagia most often refers to the dog eating his own faeces, a dog may likely eat that of another animal as well if he comes across it. Vets have found that diets with a low digestibility, containing relatively low levels of fibre and high levels of starch, increase coprophagia. Therefore, high-fibre diets may decrease the likelihood of dogs eating faeces. Both the consistency of the stool (how firm it feels in the dog's mouth) and the presence of undigested nutrients increase the likelihood. Dogs often find the stool of cats and horses more palatable than that

of other dogs. Once the dog develops diarrhoea from faeces eating, it will likely quit this distasteful habit, since dogs tend to prefer eating harder faeces.

To discourage this behaviour, first make sure that the food you are feeding your dog is nutritionally complete and that he is getting enough food. If changes in his diet do not seem to work, and no medical cause can be found, you will have to modify the behaviour through environmental control before it becomes a habit. There are some tricks you can try, such as adding an unpleasant-tasting substance to the faeces to make them unpalatable or adding something to the dog's food which will make it unpleasant tasting after it passes through the dog. The best way to prevent your dog from eating his stool is to make it unavailable—clean up after he eliminates and remove any stool from the garden. If it is not there, he cannot eat it.

Never reprimand the dog for stool eating, as this rarely impresses the dog. Vets recommend distracting the dog while he is in the act of stool eating. Another option is to muzzle the dog when he is in the garden to relieve himself; this usually is effective within 30 to 60 days. Coprophagia most frequently is seen in pups 6 to 12 months of age, and usually disappears around the dog's first birthday.

GLOSSARY

This glossary is intended to help you, the Rottweiler owner, better understand the specific terms used in this book as well as other terms that might surface in discussions with your veterinary surgeon during his care of your Rottweiler.

Abscess a pus-filled inflamed area of body tissue.

Acral lick granuloma unexplained licking of an area, usually the leg, that prevents healing of original wound.

Acute disease a disease whose onset is sudden and fast.

Albino an animal totally lacking in pigment (always white).

Allergy a known sensitivity that results from exposure to a given allergen.

Alopecia lack of hair.

Amaurosis an unexplained blindness from the retina.

Anaemia red-blood-cell deficiency.

Arthritis joint inflammation.

Atopic dermatitis congenital-allergen-caused inflammation of the skin.

Atrophy wasting away caused by faulty nutrition; a reduction in size.

Bloat gastric dilatation.

Calculi mineral 'stone' located in a vital organ, i.e., gall bladder.

Cancer a tumour that continues to expand and grow rapidly.

Carcinoma cancerous growth in the skin.

Cardiac arrhythmia irregular heartbeat.

Cardiomyopathy heart condition involving the septum and flow of blood.

Cartilage strong but pliable body tissue.

Cataract clouding of the eye lens.

Cherry eye third eyelid prolapsed gland.

Cleft palate improper growth of the two hard palates of the mouth.

Collie eye anomaly congenital defect of the back of the eye.

Congenital not the same as hereditary, but present at birth.

Congestive heart failure fluid buildup in lungs due to heart's inability to pump.

Conjunctivitis inflammation of the membrane that lines eyelids and eyeball.

Cow hocks poor rear legs that point inward; always incorrect.

Cryptorchid male animal with only one or both testicles undescended.

Cushing's disease condition caused by adrenal gland producing too much corticosteroid.

Cyst uninflamed swelling contain non-pus-like fluid.

Degeneration deterioration of tissue.

Demodectic mange red-mite infestation caused by *Demodex canis.*

Dermatitis skin inflammation.

Dew claw a functionless digit found on the inside of a dog's leg.

Diabetes insipidus disease of the hypothalamus gland resulting in animal passing great amounts of diluted urine.

Diabetes mellitus excess of glucose in blood stream.

Distemper contagious viral disease of dogs that can be most deadly.

Distichiasis double layer of eyelashes on an eyelid.

Dysplasia abnormal, poor development of a body part, especially a joint.

Dystrophy inherited degeneration.

Eclampsia potentially deadly disease in post-partum bitches due to calcium deficiency.

Ectropion outward turning of the eyelid; opposite of entropion.

Eczema inflammatory skin disease, marked by itching.

Edema fluid accumulation in a specific area.

Entropion inward turning of the eyelid.

Epilepsy chronic disease of the nervous system characterized by seizures.

Exocrine pancreatic insufficiency body's inability to produce enough enzymes to aid digestion.

False pregnancy pseudo-pregnancy, bitch shows all signs of pregnancy but there is no fertilization.

Follicular mange demodectic mange.

Gastric dilatation bloat caused by the dog's swallowing air resulting in distended, twisted stomach.

Gastroenteritis stomach or intestinal inflammation.

Gingivitis gum inflammation caused by plaque buildup.

Glaucoma increased eye pressure affecting vision.

Haematemesis vomiting blood.

Haematoma blood-filled swollen area.

Haematuria blood in urine.

Haemophilia bleeding disorder due to lack of clotting factor.

Haemorrhage bleeding.

Heat stroke condition due to over-heating of an animal.

Heritable an inherited condition.

Hot spot moist eczema characterised by dog's licking in same area.

Hyperglycemia excess glucose in blood.

Hypersensitivity allergy.

Hypertrophic cardiomyopathy left-ventricle septum becomes thickened and obstructs blood flow to heart.

Hypertrophic osteodystrophy condition affecting normal bone development.

Hypothyroidism disease caused by insufficient thyroid hormone.

Hypertrophy increased cell size resulting in enlargement of organ.

Hypoglycemia glucose deficiency in blood.

Idiopathic disease of unknown cause.

IgA deficiency immunoglobin deficiency resulting in digestive, breathing and skin problems.

Inbreeding mating two closely related animals, eg, mother—son.

Inflammation the changes that occur to a tissue after injury, characterised by swelling, redness, pain, etc.

Jaundice yellow colouration of mucous membranes.

Keratoconjunctivitis sicca dry eye.

Leukaemia malignant disease characterised by white blood cells released into blood stream.

Lick granuloma excessive licking of a wound, preventing proper healing.

Merle coat colour that is diluted.

Monorchid a male animal with only one testicle descended.

Neuritis nerve inflammation.

Nicitating membrane third eyelid pulling across the eye.

Nodular dermatofibrosis lumps on toes and legs, usually associated with cancer of kidney and uterus.

Osteochondritis bone or cartilage inflammation.

Outcrossing mating two breed representatives from different families.

Pancreatitis pancreas inflammation.

Pannus chronic superficial keratitis, affecting pigment and blood vessels of cornea.

Panosteitis inflammation of leg bones, characterised by lameness.

Papilloma wart.

Patellar luxation slipped kneecap, common in small dogs.

Patent ductus arteriosus an open blood vessel between pulmonary artery and aorta.

Penetrance frequency in which a trait shows up in offspring of animals carrying that inheritable trait.

Periodontitis acute or chronic inflammation of tissue surround the tooth.

Pneumonia lung inflammation.

Progressive retinal atrophy congenital disease of retina causing blindness.

Pruritis persistent itching.

Retinal atrophy thin retina.

Seborrhea dry scurf or excess oil deposits on the skin.

Stomatitis mouth inflammation.

Tumour solid or fluid-filled swelling resulting from abnormal growth.

Uremia waste product buildup in blood due to disease of kidneys.

Uveitis inflammation of the iris.

Von Willebrand's disease hereditary bleeding disease.

Wall eye lack of colour in the iris.

Weaning separating the mother from her dependent, nursing young.

Zoonosis animal disease communicable to humans.

INDEX

Page numbers in boldface indicate illustrations.

My Rottweiler

PUT YOUR PUPPY'S FIRST PICTURE HERE

Dog's Name ___TARA___ Handsome Harley___

Date _____ Photographer _____